DESIRING
GOD'S OWN HEART

KAY ARTHUR
WITH DAVID ARTHUR

HARVEST HOUSE PUBLISHERS
Eugene, Oregon 97402

Cover illustration and interior art by Micha'el Washer
Cover by Left Coast Design, Portland, Oregon

The International Inductive Study Series
DESIRING GOD'S OWN HEART

Copyright © 1997 by Precept Ministries
Published by Harvest House Publishers
Eugene, Oregon 97402

Library of Congress Cataloging-in-Publication Data

Arthur, Kay, 1933–
    Desiring God's own heart / Kay Arthur with David Arthur.
      p. cm. — (The international inductive study series)
    Includes bibliographical references.
    ISBN 1-56507-385-1
    1. Bible. O.T. Samuel—Study and teaching. 2. Bible. O.T.
Kings—Study and teaching. 3. Bible O.T. Chronicles—Study and teaching.
I. Arthur, David, 1967– . II. Title. III. Series: Arthur, Kay, 1933–
International inductive study series.
    BS1325.5.A77   1997   96-40300
    222'.4'007— dc21   CIP

Printed in the United States of America.

00   01   02   03   /   BP   /   11   10   9   8   7   6   5   4

CONTENTS

How to Get Started...

Unless details appeal to you or unless you are a methodical person, reading directions is sometimes difficult and hardly ever enjoyable! Most often, you just want to get started. Only if all else fails are you ready to tackle the instructions! We understand—we're not into details either. But read "How to Get Started" before you begin ... believe us, it will help! It is a vital part of getting started on the right foot! The pages are few and will help you immensely.

FIRST

As you study the books of 1 and 2 Samuel and 1 Chronicles, you will need four things in addition to this book:

1. A Bible you are willing to mark in. Marking is essential because it is an integral part of the learning process and will help you remember and retain what you learned. An ideal Bible for this purpose is *The International Inductive Study Bible (IISB)*. The *IISB,* which is available in the NAS or the NIV versions, comes in a single-column text format with large, easy-to-read type, and is ideal for marking. The page margins are wide and blank for note-taking.

The *IISB* also has instructions for studying each book of the Bible, but it does not contain any commentary on the text. The *IISB* isn't compiled from any particular theological stance since its purpose is to teach you how to discern truth for yourself through the inductive method of study. (The various charts and maps that you will find in this study guide are taken from the *IISB*.) Whatever Bible you use, just know you will want to mark in it, which brings us to the second item you will need.

2. A fine-point, four-color ballpoint pen or various colored fine-point pens (such as Micron pens) for writing in your Bible. The Micron pens are best for this purpose. Office supply stores should have these.

3. Colored pencils or an eight-color Pentel pencil.

4. A composition notebook or loose-leaf notebook for working on your assignments and recording your insights.

SECOND

1. As you study 1 and 2 Samuel and 1 Chronicles, you'll find specific instructions for each day's study. The study should take you between 20 and 30 minutes a day. However, if you desire to spend more time than this, you will increase your intimacy with the Word of God and the God of the Word. If you are doing this study within the framework of a class and you find the lessons too heavy, then simply do what you can. To do a little is better than to do nothing. Don't be an "all or nothing" person when it comes to Bible study.

Any time you get into the Word of God, you enter into more intensive warfare with the devil. Why? Every piece of the Christian's armor is related to the Word of God. And the enemy doesn't want you prepared for battle. Thus, the warfare! Remember that our one and only offensive weapon is the sword of the Spirit, which is the Word of God, and it is enough to fell the enemy.

To study or not to study is a matter of choice first, discipline second. It is a matter of the heart . . . on what or whom are you setting your heart? Get armed for war! And remember, victory is certain.

2. As you read each chapter, train yourself to think through the content of the text by asking the "5 W's and an

H": who, what, when, where, why, and how. Posing questions like these and searching out the answers helps you see exactly what the Word of God is saying. When you interrogate the text with the 5 W's and an H, you ask questions like these:

    a. **What** is the chapter about?
    b. **Who** are the main characters?
    c. **When** does this event or teaching take place?
    d. **Where** does this happen?
    e. **Why** is this being done or said?
    f. **How** did this happen?

3. The "when" of events or teachings is very important and should be marked in an easily recognizable way in your Bible. We do this by putting a clock (like the one shown here) in the margin of our Bibles beside the verse where the time phrase occurs. Or you may want to underline references to time in one specific color. As a reminder, note on your key word bookmark (which is explained next in this section) that you need to mark time references in each chapter.

4. You will be told about certain key words that would be wise to mark throughout this study. This is the purpose of the colored pencils and the colored pen. If you will develop the habit of marking your Bible, you will find it will make a significant difference in the effectiveness of your study and in how much you retain as a result of your study.

A **key word** is an important word that is used by the author repeatedly in order to convey his message to his reader. Certain key words will show up throughout the book, while other key words will be concentrated in specific chapters or segments of the book. When you mark a key word, you should also mark its synonyms (words that mean the same thing in the context) and its pronouns (*he, his, she, her, it, we, they, us, our, you, their, them*) in the same way you have marked the key word. Because some people have requested them, we will give you various ideas and suggestions in your daily assignments for how you can mark different key words.

Marking words for easy identification can be done by colors, symbols, or a combination of colors and symbols. However, colors are easier to distinguish than symbols. If you use symbols, we suggest you keep them very simple. For example, one of the key words in these books is **king**. You could draw a crown like this **king** over the word. If a symbol is used in marking a key word, it is best for the symbol to convey the meaning of the word.

When we mark the members of the Godhead (which we do not always mark), we color every reference to the Father, Son, and Holy Spirit in yellow. We then use a purple pen and mark the Father with a triangle, symbolizing the Trinity. Then playing off the triangle and using the purple pen, we mark the Son this way: **Jesus**, and the Holy Spirit this way: **Spirit**. If you learn to mark every reference to the Spirit, as you will see in the books you are about to study, you will begin to collect some valuable insights on the Spirit of God. However, we find that when you mark every reference to God and to Jesus your Bible becomes cluttered. Therefore, we suggest you mark these only in specific incidences.

As you begin this new venture, we would recommend that you also devise a color-coding system for marking key words that you decide to mark throughout your Bible. Then when you glance at the pages of your Bible, you will have instant recognition of the words.

When you start marking key words, it is easy to forget how you are marking them. Therefore, we recommend you cut a three-by-five card in half lengthwise and write the key words on that. Mark the words in the way you plan to mark each in the Bible text and then use the card as a bookmark. It might be good to make one bookmark for words you are marking throughout your Bible and a different one for any specific book of the Bible you are studying. Or record your marking system for the words you plan to mark throughout your Bible on a blank page in your Bible.

5. Because locations are important in a historical or biographical book of the Bible (1 and 2 Samuel and 1 Chronicles are historical books), you will find it helpful to mark locations in a distinguishable way in your study. Try double underlining every reference to a location in green (grass and trees are green!). Maps are included in this study so you can look up the locations in order to put yourself into context geographically. We suggest that you make a note on your key word bookmark to mark locations.

6. Charts called 1 SAMUEL AT A GLANCE, 2 SAMUEL AT A GLANCE, and 1 CHRONICLES AT A GLANCE are located at the end of their respective studies. When you complete your study of each chapter of a book, record the main theme of that chapter on the appropriate chart under the chapter number. The main theme of a chapter is the topic, event, or subject that the chapter deals with the most. Usually in historical or biographical books, the chapter themes center on events.

If you will develop the habit of filling out the AT A GLANCE charts as you progress through the study, you will have a complete synopsis of the book when you finish. If you have an *International Inductive Study Bible,* you will find the same chart in your Bible. If you record your chapter themes on the charts in your Bible, you'll always have them for ready reference.

7. Begin your study with prayer. Don't start without it. Why? Well, although you are doing your part to handle the Word of God accurately, remember that the Bible is a divinely inspired book. The words you are reading are absolute truth, given to you by God so you can know Him and His ways more intimately. These truths are divinely understood.

Listen: "For to us God revealed *them* through the Spirit; for the Spirit searches all things, even the depths of God. For who among men knows the *thoughts* of a man except the spirit of the man, which is in him? Even so the *thoughts* of God no one knows except the Spirit of God" (1 Corinthians 2:10,11).

This is why you need to pray. Simply tell God you want to understand His Word so you can live accordingly. Nothing pleases Him more than obedience—honoring Him as God—as you are about to see.

8. Each day when you finish your lesson, take some time to think about what you read, what you saw with your own eyes. Ask your heavenly Father how you can apply these insights, principles, precepts, and commands to your own life. At times, depending on how God speaks to you through His Word, you might want to record these "Lessons for Life" in the margin of your Bible next to the text you have studied. Simply put "LFL" in the margin of your Bible, and then, as briefly as possible, record the lesson for life that you want to remember. You can also make the note "LFL" on your key word bookmark as a reminder to look for these when you study. You will find them encouraging . . . sometimes convicting . . . in the days following when you come across them again.

THIRD

This study is designed so that you have an assignment for every day of the week. This puts you where you should be—in the Word of God on a daily basis. If you will do your study daily, you will find it more profitable than doing a week's study in one sitting. Pacing yourself in this way allows time for thinking through what you learn on a daily basis! However, whatever it takes to get it done, do it!

The seventh day of each week has several features that differ from the other six days. These features are designed to aid in one-on-one discipleship, group discussions, and Sunday school classes. However, they are profitable even if you are studying this book by yourself.

The "seventh" day is whatever day in the week you choose to finish your week's study. On this day, you will find a verse or two for you to memorize and *STORE IN YOUR HEART*. This will help you focus on a major truth or truths covered in your study that week.

To assist those using the material in a Sunday school class or a group Bible study, there are *QUESTIONS FOR DISCUSSION OR INDIVIDUAL STUDY*. Whatever your situation, seeking to answer these questions will help you reason through some key issues in the study.

If you are using the study in a group setting, make sure the answers given are supported from the Bible text itself. This practice will help ensure that you are handling the Word of God accurately. As you learn to see what the text says, you will find that the Bible explains itself.

Always examine your insights by carefully observing the text to see what it *says*. Then, before you decide what the passage of Scripture *means,* make sure you interpret it in the light of its context. Context is what goes with the text . . . the Scriptures preceding and following what is written. Scripture will never contradict Scripture. If it ever seems to contradict the rest of the Word of God, you can be certain that something is being taken out of context. If you come to a passage that is difficult to understand, reserve your interpretations for a time when you can study the passage in greater depth.

The purpose of a *THOUGHT FOR THE WEEK* is to help you apply what you've learned. We've done this for your edification. You can determine how valuable it is.

Remember, books in *The International Inductive Study Series* are survey courses. If you want to do a more in-depth study of a particular book of the Bible, we suggest you do a Precept upon Precept Bible Study Course on that book. The Precept studies are awesome but require five hours of personal study a week. However, you will never learn more! They are top-of-the-line! You may obtain more information on these courses by filling out and mailing the response card in the back of this book.

FIRST
SAMUEL

What Will It Take for You to Give God Your Heart?

Have you ever desired something so strongly that you felt you would be ill without it? Have you ever wanted a relationship with someone so badly that you thought you would die if you couldn't have it?

Oh, to long with that same intensity for a personal relationship with the living God! To be willing to pay the price to know Him by spending time in His Word, for there you learn His ways and His character! How pleasing this would be to our God, for He longs deeply to have you know Him, to understand His heart, to walk in His ways.

In this week's lesson, you will encounter people who sought God and others who were unwilling to discipline themselves for the purpose of godliness. Don't miss what you can learn by observing each.

DAY ONE

Since Samuel, Kings, and Chronicles are historical books, it is important to understand where they fit in the history of Israel. First Samuel closes the period of the judges and marks the beginning of the period of the kings of Israel. This transition is evident since 1 Samuel opens with an account of the life of Samuel, the last judge of Israel, and then leads into the days of the kings as recorded in the books of 1 and 2 Samuel, 1 and 2 Kings, and 1 and 2 Chronicles. The diagram below will give you a visual picture of the historical parallel of Samuel, Kings, and Chronicles.

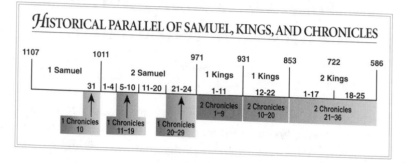

HISTORICAL PARALLEL OF SAMUEL, KINGS, AND CHRONICLES

Although our study will focus primarily on the books of 1 and 2 Samuel, we will incorporate parallel passages from 1 Chronicles which will give you the complete picture of the times and events you are studying.

Historical books, while documenting facts, offer revolutionary insights into God, into people, and into how man and God relate in the varied circumstances of life. As you follow the lives of the Israelites during the period of Samuel, we pray that you will desire a deeper relationship with God and that the knowledge of His character and His ways will leave you longing to know more of Him.

Begin your study of 1 Samuel today by reading chapter 1. Concentrate on the *who* and the *what* of the 5 W's and an H (refer to "How to Get Started" on page 5). Then in your notebook, list what this chapter is about—the events that take place in 1 Samuel 1 and the main characters who are involved in these events.

DAY TWO

If you have not read the "How to Get Started" section in the front of this book, it would be beneficial to do so before you go any further. That section explains the how and why of inductive Bible study. Now would also be a good time to stop and begin a key word bookmark to use throughout your study of 1 and 2 Samuel and 1 Chronicles. (Again, if you have questions, refer to the "How To Get Started" section.)

As you saw yesterday, three main characters emerge in this first chapter: *Hannah, Eli,* and *Samuel.* As you read today, note what you learn about these three people by marking references to each with a distinguishable color or symbol. Remember to mark the synonyms and/or pronouns relating to each character in the same distinctive way. Marking references to these people will reveal what each character does, what has happened in his or her past, what is currently happening, or what will happen in the future. Also, don't miss marking references to Samuel as a child.

Hannah's name occurs only in the first two chapters, but she is a key person in Samuel's life. In chapters 1–4, you will mark Eli's name. However, since Hannah's and Eli's names are mentioned only in the early chapters, don't add them to your bookmark. *Samuel* is a main character throughout, so his name will be the first key word you will want to put on your bookmark.

After you read chapter 1 and mark the three main characters, you will find it helpful to record in your notebook what you observe about each of these people. Therefore, make a list about each person. Leave enough room to add to the list on Eli through chapter 4. Samuel is the central character of this study, so you will want to leave several pages for the list about him. Also, as you write down your observations throughout this study, you will find it helpful to put the Scripture verse where you find the information next to the observation so that you can see easily where you found your information.

When you have completed your assignment, review what you observed in the lives of Hannah, Eli, and Samuel and think how you can apply any of this to your life. Record any "Lessons for Life" (LFL) in the margin of your Bible or in your notebook. (If you are unfamiliar with the term LFL, see the "How to Get Started" section.)

Finally, identify the theme of this chapter. Record the theme on the appropriate line of the 1 SAMUEL AT A GLANCE chart on page 62 or make a larger version of the chart in your notebook and fill it out as you go along. If you have an *IISB*, don't forget to fill in your information there too.

DAY THREE

Read 1 Samuel 2:1-10 and mark every reference to the LORD (including synonyms, such as *God* and pronouns such as *He* or *Thy*[1]). Note what you learn about God in these first ten verses and begin a list in your notebook where you can continue to record insights about God.

As you read, notice how Hannah's prayer relates to her situation. This prayer is packed with lessons for life. Be sure to write in the margin of your Bible or in your notes any "LFL" that you discover.

DAY FOUR

Today you are going to read and mark 1 Samuel 2:11-36. Add to your key word bookmark *sin*[2]*(s)* and any synonyms such as *evil things.*[3] Later you will mark other synonyms such as *sinned,*[4] *sinning, transgression,*[5] *transgressed,*[6] and *iniquity,*[7] so add these to your bookmark now also.

As you have done previously, note what this chapter teaches you about Samuel. Then note specifically how Eli's sons, Hophni and Phinehas, sinned. Mark every reference to these two men and record what you learn about them in your notebook. Leviticus 7:22-25 is an excellent cross-reference with 1 Samuel 2:12-17, so you might want to write "Leviticus 7:22-25" next to this passage in 1 Samuel. Cross-referencing helps you remember the location of a passage that sheds light on or correlates with the one you are studying. Cross-referencing is also very helpful when you don't have your study notes, because your notes are right in your Bible!

DAY FIVE

Read 1 Samuel 2:11-36 and focus on what you learn from this chapter about Eli. Look for the 5 W's and an H. Note who interacts with Eli, what he tells him, and why. Add all your insights to your list on Samuel.

Identify the theme of chapter 2 and record it on the 1 SAMUEL AT A GLANCE chart on page 62.

DAY SIX

Today read 1 Samuel 3 and mark every reference, including pronouns, to the *Lord*, to *Samuel,* and to *Eli.* Add to your lists what you learn about the character and behavior of both Samuel and Eli. Be sure to note on your list about Eli what God reveals to Samuel about him. Also note what you see about God in this chapter. As you mark your key words, don't miss the word *iniquity*.[8]

Note how and why God is going to judge Eli and his household. Examine the reasons carefully and record any new insights on Eli in your notebook.

Identify and record the theme of chapter 3 on the 1 SAMUEL AT A GLANCE chart on page 62.

DAY SEVEN

Store in your heart: 1 Samuel 2:2.

Read and discuss: 1 Samuel 2:1-17; 2:29; 3:12,13; Leviticus 7:22-25.

QUESTIONS FOR DISCUSSION OR INDIVIDUAL STUDY

∾ At what point in Israel's history does 1 Samuel begin? (Refer to Day One for help.)

∾ Describe the sequence of events that occurs in 1 Samuel 1–2 as it relates to Hannah's request for a son.

∾ What did you learn about God from Hannah's prayer in 1 Samuel 2:1-10?

  a. What does this tell you about Hannah?

  b. How does knowing God affect your prayer life?

∾ What reason did God give for judging Eli and his house (2:29; 3:12,13)?

  a. What was Eli's responsibility regarding his sons? Was he accountable to God for them?

  b. What had Eli's sons done to deserve this kind of punishment (2:12-17)?

c. How important was it for Eli to follow God's instructions regarding the offerings and sacrifices? Discuss what you saw in Leviticus 7:22-25.

∾ What do you learn from this week's lesson that would apply to the role of parents in relation to their children, especially fathers?

THOUGHT FOR THE WEEK

In these first three chapters of 1 Samuel, you have seen the sharp contrast between Hannah and her son, Samuel, and Eli and his sons, Hophni and Phinehas. In 1 Samuel 2:35, God says that He will raise up a faithful priest who will do according to what is in His heart and in His soul . . . and that He will build him an enduring house. Eli was not this kind of man . . . and thus his house was judged forever. God put Eli's sons to death not only because of their sin but because their father failed to rebuke them. In essence, Eli compromised his priesthood.

Ironically, the very woman Eli rebuked, thinking her drunk, was the woman who, through faith and perseverance, would receive a son who would say to God, "Speak, LORD, for Thy servant is listening" (1 Samuel 3:9).

When we become children of God, we become part of a kingdom of priests unto God. Will you be a faithful priest doing what is in God's heart and soul rather than living according to what is in your own?

If you want an "enduring house"—a family who will follow in your footsteps—this is where you begin. Listen to God and do all that He says.

When the Glory
of the LORD Departs...

Do you think that we as human beings have a tendency to forget just how holy God is? This week, our study on the ark of the covenant will be a reminder of the fact that God is to be treated as holy.

DAY ONE

Read 1 Samuel 4 and give attention to the following:

1. Israel's adversarial encounter with the Philistines. This is a major subject throughout the book of 1 Samuel. Therefore, watch the references to the *Philistines*. You may want to record what you learn about them in your notebook.

It is interesting to note that although the land of Israel is often referred to as "Palestine," the word is not used as such in the Bible. Palestine is a reference to the land of the Philistines, the southeastern coastal strip along the Mediterranean, that is, where Gaza is now.

2. *The ark of the covenant.* Add *the ark of God (the ark of the covenant of the LORD,*[9] *the ark of the covenant of God, the ark of the LORD)* to your bookmark. The ark plays a key role in the life of the Israelites. Mark the references to the ark, then go back and mark *the ark of God* in 1 Samuel 3:3. Also mark any pronouns that refer to the ark.

In your notebook, start a list of what you learn about the ark. Be sure to note events such as where the ark is taken, why, what happens as a result of it, and how long it remains in each of these various places.

3. *Eli.* As you add to your list on *Eli*, note the cause of his death and then reflect on what you've observed about his life.

4. *Ichabod.* Note the birth of *Ichabod* and why he is given this name.

Don't forget to record the theme of chapter 4 on the 1 SAMUEL AT A GLANCE chart.

DAY TWO

Today read 1 Samuel 5 and mark every reference, including pronouns, to *the ark of God*[10] *(the ark of the LORD, the ark of the God of Israel).* In your notebook, add to your list any new insights you discover about the ark.

When the ark was taken from the Israelites, it was said "the glory has departed from Israel" (1 Samuel 4:22). What was the ark of God? Why was it so special? Look at a description of the ark: The ark, a box 4 feet long by 2½ feet wide by 2½ feet high, was constructed of acacia wood and overlaid with gold inside and out. Because it symbolized God's presence, no one was allowed to touch it. Four gold rings were attached to the feet of the ark. Poles, made of acacia wood and overlaid with gold, were slipped through these rings so that the ark could be carried from place to place (Exodus 25:10-22). Only the Kohathites (a division of the Levites) were allowed to move the ark.

When the ark was in the tabernacle, the cloud of God's presence hovered over the mercy seat (Leviticus

16:2; 1 Samuel 4:4). The mercy seat, made of pure gold with a gold cherub attached at each end, covered the ark of the covenant. On the day of atonement the high priest sprinkled the blood of sacrifice on the mercy seat as a covering for the sins of the people. (The Hebrew word for "mercy" is *kapporeth,* meaning "a covering.")

Inside the ark was the testimony, the stone tablets bearing the ten commandments (Exodus 40:20; Deuteronomy 10:2). For a period of time, the ark also contained Aaron's rod which budded (Numbers 17:10) and a gold jar of manna (Hebrews 9:4).[11]

The ark was first housed in the tabernacle and later in the temple. God told Moses to place the ark of the covenant in the Holy of Holies and promised: "And there I will meet with you; and from above the mercy seat, from between the two cherubim which are upon the ark of the testimony, I will speak to you about all that I will give you in commandment for the sons of Israel" (Exodus 25:22).

The ark represented the throne of God. It was within the Holy of Holies that God met with man. Only the high priest could enter the Holy of Holies once a year—on the day of atonement.

DAY THREE

Today read 1 Samuel 5 again. On the map on the next page trace the journeys of the ark as recorded in this chapter.

Record in your notebook what you learn about God in this chapter as it relates to the ark of God.

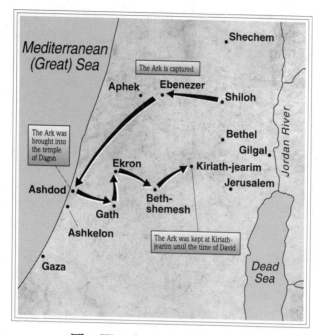

The Wanderings of the Ark

Note specifically what happens when the Philistines take the ark of God into the house of Dagon. Also observe what happens to those who have the ark in their custody.

> Dagon was the chief deity worshiped by the Philistines. Ancient Canaanite literature records that he was the father of the god, Baal.

During this time in history, it was a common practice for the head and hands of a defeated army's leader to be cut off and given to the conquering nation.

Identify the theme of 1 Samuel 5 and record it on the 1 SAMUEL AT A GLANCE chart.

Day Four

Continue to track the movement of *the ark of the Lord* as you read 1 Samuel 6. Mark every reference to *the ark*. You may want to add to your list in your notebook any pertinent facts you learn about the ark of the Lord as you evaluate them in your study.

Look for and mark any key words such as *evil* (a synonym of *sin*). Also double underline any geographic locations since marking the locations will help you to follow the movement of the ark. Then continue to trace the movements of the ark on the map as you did yesterday. Marking time references will help you keep everything in context.

As you continue to add to your list on the ark, don't forget to record the effects the ark had on the different people who encountered it. Did it affect only non-Israelites? Or was God non-partial with His judgments?

Remember to put the theme of chapter 6 on the 1 SAM-UEL AT A GLANCE chart and make a note of any LFL you can apply to your life.

Day Five

Today read 1 Samuel 7 and mark all the geographic locations. Mark and continue to trace the journey of *the ark* on your map. Mark any other key words that are noted on your bookmark.

Day Six

In 1 Samuel 7:3, note the list of instructions Samuel gives to the house of Israel. Also note what God will do if they obey. You may want to number each of these instructions as they are listed in your Bible.

Record in your notebook the various things Samuel and the children of Israel do in response to God's promise to deliver them if they obey. Also note the sign set up by Samuel and its significance.

Add to your list any new insights you glean regarding Samuel. This is the chapter that tells us that Samuel was a judge.

Study the chart below to determine where Samuel's judgeship fits into the history of Israel's judges.

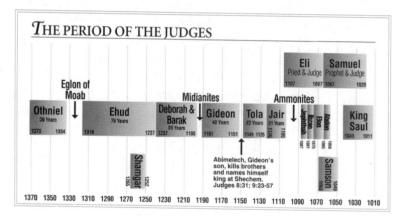

THE PERIOD OF THE JUDGES

Identify the theme of this chapter and record it on the 1 SAMUEL AT A GLANCE chart.

DAY SEVEN

Store in your heart: 1 Samuel 7:3.
Read and discuss: 1 Samuel 4:1-22; 7:5-11, 19-21.

QUESTIONS FOR DISCUSSION OR INDIVIDUAL STUDY

Read 1 Samuel 4:1-22. What was the outcome of the first battle with the Philistines as mentioned in chapter 4?

∾ By what means did the elders of Israel attempt to achieve a different outcome for the next battle?

   a. On what were they relying to save them? What was the result?

   b. What events followed this second battle?

∾ Read 1 Samuel 7:5-11. Prior to this battle, what steps did Israel take that caused this battle to differ from previous battles?

∾ What had changed?

∾ Discuss the course of action taken by Samuel and the Israelites.

∾ What was the outcome of this battle?

∾ Why do you think this battle ended differently than the previous battles?

∾ In 1 Samuel 7:19-21 several Israelites lose their lives as they look into the ark. Why? What do you learn about the character of God from this event?

∾ Summarize what you learned about the ark of the covenant and the holiness of God this week. How can you apply this to your own life?

Thought for the Week

In our study this week we saw the mention of two words: Ichabod and Ebenezer. These words are easy to remember and yet full of significance. Commit them to memory and be challenged in your walk with the Lord.

Remember that your body is the temple of the Holy Spirit who is in you and that you are not your own. You have been bought with a price. Therefore, glorify God in your body. Let no man say of you, "Ichabod." Be careful that you do not set up any idols in your life but "that you serve the LORD alone."

If you will remember this and walk in obedience then you too can erect a stone, name it *Ebenezer,* and say with confidence, "thus far the LORD has helped [me]" (1 Samuel 7:12).

Who Do You Want to Rule over You... God or Man?

Have you ever thought, "I don't need God's help. I can fix it myself!" Maybe you feel God is distant and uninvolved in your life. Or possibly you have concluded that it doesn't really matter to God how you deal with the issues in your life. Therefore, you have decided to solve your problems in your own way.

For over three hundred years, Israel was ruled by judges raised up by God. Now the tide is about to turn.

This week as you read 1 Samuel 8–11, ask God what lessons He has for you as you study these chapters.

DAY ONE

Read Judges 2:6-19 in order to establish the historical context of the chapters that you will study this week. Then read 1 Samuel 8 and mark every occurrence of the word *king*, including pronouns, and add the word to your bookmark. You might simply want to draw a crown over the word like this: **king** .

A pivotal point in the history of the children of Israel occurs in 1 Samuel 8:7. God says to Samuel, "They have not rejected you, but they have rejected Me from being king over them." If you are studying in the *King James Version* or the *New King James Version*, this phrase is translated "that I should not reign over them." We don't want you to miss what God is saying, so mark the word *reign* in this instance in the same way you have marked *king*.

DAY TWO

Read 1 Samuel 8:1-5 and record in your notebook the problem facing Israel and the solution proposed by the elders of Israel. Then read 1 Samuel 8:19,20 and list the people's reasons for insisting on a king.

Finally read through this chapter again and mark the word *take*. Observe what the king will take from the people. Number these things right in the text of your Bible. Also note the consequences of such a choice as stated in verse 18.

Identify the theme of 1 Samuel 8 and record it on the 1 SAMUEL AT A GLANCE chart.

DAY THREE

Before delving into today's lesson, add *Saul* to your bookmark. Make certain to mark this word, along with any pronouns that refer to him, in the same distinctive way. As you mark the references to God's Spirit in this chapter, do not confuse them with any mention of other spirits.

Now read 1 Samuel 9 and mark the key words. Also mark *man of God* (and any pronouns or synonyms that refer to him), but do not add the phrase to your bookmark. Who is the *man of God*?

If you gain any new insights on Samuel, record them in your notebook. Also note what you learn about Saul from this chapter.

Identify the theme of 1 Samuel 9 and record it on the 1 SAMUEL AT A GLANCE.

Day Four

Read 1 Samuel 10:1-16.

Add the phrase *Spirit of the LORD* to your bookmark, then go through these verses again and mark the key words and other information from your bookmark. Watch the role God plays in the anointing of Saul and the role Saul plays.

In 1 Samuel 10:8 be sure to mark the critical time phrase so it stands out in your text.

An interesting item to note is the mention of "high place" in verse 13. The "high place" is where the priests went to worship God. As described in other books of the Old Testament, ungodly men also built high places for idol worship to foreign gods.

Finally, add to your lists on Samuel and Saul any insights you want to remember about them from this chapter.

Day Five

Today finish reading chapter 10. Mark the key words, locations, and references to time. Don't forget to mark *king*. Add to your bookmark the phrases *inquired (further) of the LORD*[12] or *inquired of God*[13] and mark this phrase beginning in this chapter. Note who inquires of the LORD and on what occasions. Observe the response of the people of Israel to the selection of a king and add any new insights to your list on Samuel and Saul. Be sure to see God's stand on the decision to have a king over Israel.

Identify the theme of chapter 10 and record it on the 1 SAMUEL AT A GLANCE chart.

DAY SIX

Read 1 Samuel 11 today. Add the word *covenant*[14] to your key word bookmark. However, be careful not to mark *covenant* in the same way you marked *the ark of the covenant* since this usage of the word carries a different meaning.

Mark the other key words as you read about Saul's first battle as a leader. What happens to Saul that gives him the strength to attack the enemy? Have you seen anything similar in the previous chapters? If so, write the cross references of the events next to each other in the margin of your Bible.

Add any new insights on Saul to your list in your notebook. There is an excellent map entitled SAUL'S ASCENT TO KINGSHIP on page 35 that you will appreciate after studying the first eleven chapters of 1 Samuel.

Record the theme of 1 Samuel 11 on the 1 SAMUEL AT A GLANCE chart.

DAY SEVEN

Store in your heart: 1 Samuel 8:7.
Read and discuss: 1 Samuel 8:1-22; 10:6,10: 11:6; Deuteronomy 7:16; Joshua 10:42.

QUESTIONS FOR DISCUSSION OR INDIVIDUAL STUDY

∿ What is the problem with Israel's leadership in 1 Samuel 8:1-3?

∿ What solution did the Israelites choose for themselves? Did God sanction this solution? Give the reason for your answer.

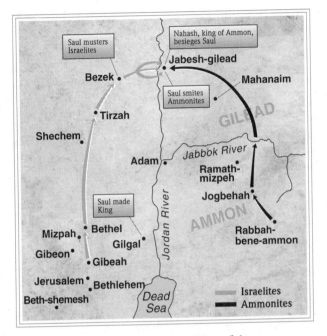

Saul's Ascent to Kingship

∾ Discuss the reasons given by the people of Israel for wanting a king to rule over them (8:5,19,20).

∾ Read Deuteronomy 7:6 and Joshua 10:42. How do these verses support or discredit Israel's reasoning?

∾ From 1 Samuel 8:10-18, discuss the consequences of having a king rule over them that Samuel cites. Did these consequences come from Samuel's own reasoning, or did they have another source besides him?

∾ The *Spirit of the Lord* or *Spirit of God* is mentioned in 1 Samuel 10:6,10 and 11:6. Discuss the events and effects of the *Spirit of God* in these passages. Be sure to keep them in the context of the passages where you find them.

∾ What kind of things or people do we inaugurate as kings in our lives in place of God's rulership?

THOUGHT FOR THE WEEK

Israel had a legitimate problem: Corrupt men were in leadership. Her problem was very real and required a sure solution. The people chose a solution based on human rationale, a solution that seemed to make sense in the eyes of the world.

Israel reasoned that a king to judge, rule, and fight for them was what the situation called for. She wanted to be like the other nations. Yet, *God* was Israel's king. Israel was warned that to establish a human monarch was to spurn God. Israel did not heed the warning but preferred visible, human flesh to an invisible God.

Do you gravitate toward solutions that display self-sufficiency, thereby setting up your own "kings"? Do you tend to seek friends, a parent, or your pastor to help solve problems before you seek God? Ask the Lord to show you whether your trust in humanity outweighs your trust in Him.

What Does God See
When He Looks at Your Heart?

What qualifies a person to be a man or woman of God? It's a matter of the heart.

DAY ONE

Read 1 Samuel 12. Mark the key words from your bookmark. Add to your list on Samuel, including any warnings Samuel gives to the children of Israel. Note Samuel's instructions to the people. What is promised as the outcome of their obedience? Evaluate your own life in light of Samuel's instructions. Are you serving the Lord with all your heart, or are you pursuing futile things which do not profit?

What is the significance of the event that takes place in verses 17,18? What was Samuel trying to show the people? The weather patterns were such that it never rained during the time of the harvest in Israel. Does knowing this fact increase your understanding of why this rain was a judgment on them?

Identify the theme of chapter 12 and record it on the 1 SAMUEL AT A GLANCE chart.

DAY TWO

Read 1 Samuel 13 and mark every reference to *Saul* and *Samuel*. Also add *Jonathan* to your bookmark and mark the references to him. (Don't forget to mark the pronouns.) When you finish reading and marking the chapter, begin a list on Jonathan. Add any new insights that you gain regarding Saul or Samuel to your lists. Don't forget to mark the time phrases and locations in this chapter.

Read 1 Samuel 10:8 and 1 Samuel 13:8-14. Compare these two references, evaluating what Samuel told Saul to do and then what Saul did. Sin always has a consequence. In this case, what were the consequences of Saul's disobedience?

Write 1 Samuel 10:8 and 1 Samuel 13:8-14 as cross-references beside one another in the margin of your Bible. In other words, note 1 Samuel 10:8 beside 13:8-14 and vice versa.

Identify the theme of 1 Samuel 13 and record it on the 1 SAMUEL AT A GLANCE chart. Are you remembering to note any LFL as you see things that you can apply to your life?

DAY THREE

Today and tomorrow you are going to look at 1 Samuel 14. Read 14:1-30 today and mark the key words from your bookmark. Jot down on your list what you learn about Jonathan in this section. Don't miss his perception of the way the Lord works. Remember to record new insights on Saul as well.

DAY FOUR

Read the rest of chapter 14 today beginning with verse 31. Be sure to mark the phrase *inquired of God*[15] as you mark the other key words from your bookmark. Make additions of any new insights to your lists on Jonathan and Saul. Note

Jonathan's relationship with God and with his father, Saul. Pay special attention to Saul's foolish oath and the events that follow.

Read the command God gave to the children of Israel in Leviticus 3:17 and compare it with 1 Samuel 14:31-35. Also note Leviticus 3:17 as a cross-reference to the verse in chapter 14 to which it pertains.

Identify the theme of this chapter and record it on the 1 SAMUEL AT A GLANCE chart.

DAY FIVE

Today read 1 Samuel 15 and mark the key words and other pertinent information. Update your lists on Saul and Samuel. Carefully consider Samuel's conversation with Saul. Notice Saul's actions and his response to Samuel. What reasons does Saul give for what he does? Does he confess his sins or shift the blame to others? Record the consequences of Saul's disobedience.

Carefully examine 1 Samuel 15:22,23. How important is obedience? What is rebellion? (Read verses 22,23 in the KJV if you have access to it.)

Identify the theme of this chapter and record it on the 1 SAMUEL AT A GLANCE chart.

DAY SIX

Before you begin to read 1 Samuel 16, add *evil spirit* and *David* to your bookmark. Consider marking every mention of David's name. Realize though that his name is prominent throughout the remainder of the book, so you may not want all those marks in the text. Also mark any other key words that you observe in this chapter.

Begin a list on David in your notebook. Leave room for insights you will add from 2 Samuel. Add fresh observations to your lists on Saul and Samuel. Remember to record the corresponding chapter and verse beside each observation in your notebook.

Now observe what the Lord looks at in 1 Samuel 16:7. Are you comforted by that thought?

Identify the theme of chapter 16 and record it on the 1 SAMUEL AT A GLANCE chart.

DAY SEVEN

Store in your heart: 1 Samuel 12:22,24 and/or 1 Samuel 15:22,23.

Read and discuss: 1 Samuel 12:12-25; 15:1-35.

QUESTIONS FOR DISCUSSION OR INDIVIDUAL STUDY

- What promises and warnings does Samuel give to the people in 1 Samuel 12:12-15?

- What did Samuel ask God to do in order to show the people the wickedness of their choice (12:17)?

- How did the people respond to this miraculous sign from God (12:18,19)?

- What does Samuel tell them to do in 1 Samuel 12:24,25?

- Discuss the sequence of events in 1 Samuel 15:1-35.

   a. What were Samuel's instructions to Saul?

   b. What was Saul's response?

   c. What were the consequences?

   d. What truth did you learn about obedience in this chapter?

∾ What have you learned about "partial obedience"? How do you think God feels about it in our lives?

THOUGHT FOR THE WEEK

Does it ever hit you that God's grace is sufficient? Have there been days, weeks, perhaps even months in your life when you felt you had blown it with God? Why does a holy and righteous God continue to put up with us? Why does the Creator of the universe continue to love us even when we mess up?

The nation of Israel basically had said to God's face, "We don't need You anymore! We want a king to rule over us. We want to be like the other nations." The Scripture says that they were rejecting God. In chapter 12, Samuel tells Israel that if they will fear the Lord and serve Him with all their hearts that the all-powerful hand of God will not be against them. Sam-uel gives the people of Israel this promise: "For the LORD will not abandon His people." Why not? Why didn't God just wipe them from the face of the earth? He could have chosen another nation or even started over and created another Israel. But He didn't. God chose to show grace to His people for one reason: *"On account of His great name, because the LORD has been pleased to make you a people for Himself"* (12:22).

God assures us that He will not give up on us. If we will come back to Him and turn our hearts toward Him, His all-sufficient grace will cover our past and cleanse us from our sins. God's grace is based solely on His great name. So friend, if you have blown it with God or if you are in one of those times when you feel distant from your heavenly Father, call out to Him in humility and fear and be embraced by His ever-forgiving arms. He desires your heart to be one with His.

Swartwout - Living Springs
      Leadership

Can God Truly Make My Heart Like His? How?

Is it still possible to be a man or woman after God's own heart—like David was? Do you think you could have a relationship with God like David's? What does it take to have a heart tightly knit with God's?

This week you will see the contrast between two hearts: one given over to God and one controlled by its own will. Pay close attention to David in this week's study to gain insights on growing closer to God. Your heart *can* truly be like God's heart. Study this week to find out how.

DAY ONE

Read the story of David and Goliath in 1 Samuel 17 and see what new insights you can glean from studying it yourself. Note what you learn about David and add it to your list. Observe what it is that motivates and inspires him. Continue to mark key words from your bookmark and to update the lists in your notebook.

Identify the theme for chapter 17 and record it on the 1 SAMUEL AT A GLANCE chart.

DAY TWO

Today read 1 Samuel 18 and mark the key words. Make additions to your lists on Jonathan, David, and Saul. Be sure to mark the word *covenant* and note on your list the exchange that takes place between Jonathan and David as it relates to the covenant. Note the reason for this covenant.

Also note the way David responds to Saul in each situation. As you observe the character and actions of Saul and David, ask God to reveal to you the truth about your own character and attitude. Mark in the margin of your Bible any LFL.

Identify the theme of this chapter and record it on the 1 SAMUEL AT A GLANCE chart.

Day Three

As you read 1 Samuel 19 today, observe the relationships between Jonathan, David, and Saul. Add your observations to your lists. Be sure to mark time phrases such as *then*[16] and *when* so that you can follow the sequence of events in this chapter. As you mark key words, don't forget to mark *Spirit of God* and *evil spirit*,[17] each in its own distinctive way.

Identify the theme of chapter 19 and record it on the 1 SAMUEL AT A GLANCE chart on page 62.

Day Four

Read 1 Samuel 20. Note your insights regarding Jonathan and David and their covenant relationship. Refer back to 1 Samuel 18:1-4, which relates the account of their entering into covenant. Note in this chapter the extension of the covenant, that is, whom it includes.

Jot down what you see occurring in the hearts of Jonathan, David, and Saul on your lists. Also record their actions.

Don't forget to mark other key words such as *iniquity*[18] and *sin*.[19]

Identify the theme of 1 Samuel 20 and record it on the 1 SAMUEL AT A GLANCE chart.

DAY FIVE

Add *Achish* to your bookmark before you begin today's work. Then read 1 Samuel 21 and mark the key words. In this chapter (and in tomorrow's assignment) mark *Ahimelech* and *Doeg the Edomite*[20] and note what they do. Do not add them to your bookmark. The Edomites were among the nations that Saul and the army of Israel fought against in 1 Samuel 14:47.

Don't forget to add to your lists on Saul and David. Also begin a list on Achish.

There are several geographic locations mentioned in this chapter. Double underline each geographical location in the text and on the map, ISRAEL IN THE DAYS OF SAMUEL, SAUL, AND DAVID on page 47.

Record the theme for this chapter on the 1 SAMUEL AT A GLANCE chart.

DAY SIX

Read 1 Samuel 22 and again mark the key words. Don't miss the description of the men who joined David. Also mark *Ahimelech* and *Doeg the Edomite* and add to your lists any pertinent information you want to remember about them and about David and Saul.

Record your chapter theme on the 1 SAMUEL AT A GLANCE chart.

Day Seven

Store in your heart: 1 Samuel 17:45 or 17:47.
Read and discuss: 1 Samuel 17:1-58; 18:1-5, 20:8,12-17,42.

Questions for Discussion or Individual Study

1 Samuel 17:1-58

∾ What was David's occupation when he confronted Goliath? What was his position in the family (17:12-15)?

∾ What had David experienced in the past that gave him courage? To whom did he give the credit?

∾ Why did David want to fight Goliath (17:26,36)?

∾ What were the weapons David used against the giant (17:40)? What does he say in 1 Samuel 17:45?

∾ Discuss what David says to Goliath before the battle (17:41-47).

1 Samuel 18:1-5; 20:8, 12-17,42

∾ Discuss the first covenant made by Jonathan with David. What prompted the cutting of this covenant? What did they do when they entered into this covenant?

∾ When David feels that he may confront death at Saul's hand, what does he remind Jonathan of?

∾ Discuss the new covenant made in 1 Samuel 20:8. Note whom this is between and for how long. Who is invoked to watch over this covenant?

∾ Discuss the characteristics you observed about David in your study this week.

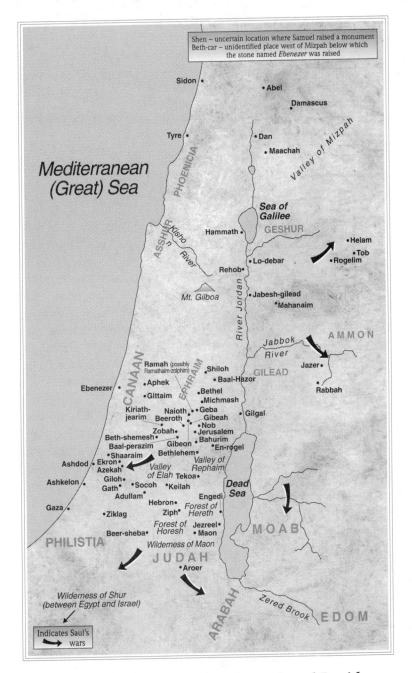

Israel in the Days of Samuel, Saul, and David

∾ Compare and contrast your lists on David and Saul from this week's observations.

∾ What can you learn from David's approach to problems as you encounter difficulties in your life?

THOUGHT FOR THE WEEK

God anointed a new man to be king over His nation, to replace Saul. He chose a shepherd boy, David, whom God called "a man after My own heart."

David knew and believed that his God was the supreme and final authority. David knew that no man could stay God's hand or say to Him, "What are You doing?" Even in his confrontation with Goliath, David recognized the vast greatness of God, who gave him victory in a seemingly impossible situation. And what was his motivation for facing Goliath? He wanted all the earth to know that there was a God in Israel.

Would God call you a man or woman after His own heart? Does your life demonstrate to all the world that there is a God who reigns in your life? From where does your strength come? Does it come from God or from man? God looks not at the outward appearance but rather at the heart. His desire is to strongly support those whose hearts are completely His. Would the people who know you best say that your heart belongs fully to God?

WEEK SIX

Are You Willing to Let God Handle Your Enemies for You?

Have you ever been presented with an opportunity to avenge yourself, to get back at someone who hurt you? Have you found yourself in a situation where you could take matters into your own hands and get immediate relief, yet at the same time knowing the relief would be by your hand and not God's?

In this week's lesson, watch David's reaction to this kind of situation. Ask God to give you His insight and understanding into how He would have you deal with your enemies.

DAY ONE

Read 1 Samuel 23 and mark the key words. As you do, note David's dependence upon God. Add your observations of David, Saul, and Jonathan to the lists in your notebook. Note what Jonathan says to David in verses 16-18. Remember to mark the geographical locations and time phrases.

Identify the theme of chapter 23 and record it on the 1 SAMUEL AT A GLANCE chart.

DAY TWO

Today read 1 Samuel 24 and mark key words and other information. Mark *rebellion*[21] in verse 11 since it is used as a synonym for *sin* in this case. Also note your observations on Saul and David.

As you add today's insights to your lists, include David's reasons for not stretching out his hand against Saul. Note Saul's confession, realization, and request of David and how David responds to him in verses 16-22. Is there any other reason why David would have made this promise? Remember David and Jonathan's covenant.

Identify the theme of 1 Samuel 24 and record it on the 1 SAMUEL AT A GLANCE chart.

DAY THREE

Read 1 Samuel 25 and mark the key words. Also mark any references to *Abigail* and *Nabal*. You may want to write the definition of the name *Nabal*—"senseless, foolish"—in the margin of your Bible next to verse 25. As you note your observations about David and add to your list, watch carefully the sequence of events. Remember to mark the geographical locations and add to your list on Saul.

Identify the theme of chapter 25 and record it on the 1 SAMUEL AT A GLANCE chart.

DAY FOUR

Read 1 Samuel 26 and mark key words, time phrases, and geographical locations. Record what you learn about David and Saul on the lists in your notebook. Include the reasons David states for sparing Saul.

Identify the theme of 1 Samuel 26 and record it on the 1 SAMUEL AT A GLANCE chart.

DAY FIVE

Read 1 Samuel 27–28. Mark key words and geographical locations. Check these locations on the map on page 47, ISRAEL IN THE DAYS OF SAMUEL, SAUL, AND DAVID. Add what you learn about Achish to your list about him. Update your list of observations on David and Saul. Note what Saul does in chapter 28 when the Lord does not answer him. What was wrong with what Saul did? (See Deuteronomy 18:10-12 for further insight.) What do you do when God does not answer according to your timetable?

Identify the themes of 1 Samuel 27 and 28 and record them on the 1 SAMUEL AT A GLANCE chart. Do you see any LFL in these chapters?

DAY SIX

Read 1 Samuel 29–30. Mark the geographical locations and follow the movements of David on the map on page 47, ISRAEL IN THE DAYS OF SAMUEL, SAUL, AND DAVID.

Read 1 Samuel 30:6 and note David's situation and where he turns for strength. Think about his situation, then think about the difficulties you have or are currently facing.

Record your insights about David, Saul, and the Philistines.

Identify the themes for chapters 29 and 30 and record them on the 1 SAMUEL AT A GLANCE chart.

DAY SEVEN

Store in your heart: 1 Samuel 26:23a.
Read and discuss: 1 Samuel 23–30.

QUESTIONS FOR DISCUSSION OR INDIVIDUAL STUDY

∾ Why wouldn't David kill Saul? Wouldn't it have been better for Saul to be out of the way so that David could assume the leadership of Israel? After all, wasn't David anointed by Samuel at God's instruction to be the leader of Israel? What statement does David make about what God will do (26:10)?

∾ Compare 1 Samuel 26:10 with 27:1. What does this tell you about David? Can you relate?

∾ Discuss any thoughts about Saul from chapters 23–30 as you consider your lists. Be sure to mention the Scripture references in order to support your statements regarding Saul.

∾ What did you learn about David from 1 Samuel 23–30? Discuss David's heart as you have seen it described in the text.

∾ After looking at the lives of Samuel, Saul, and Jonathan, what do you learn about obedience to God's instructions and about the consequences for disobedience?

THOUGHT FOR THE WEEK

Who was David most interested in pleasing? Was he seeking his own way, or was he seeking the heart of God? How about you? What are you seeking?

The attitude of David's heart set him apart from other men. David had given His God the place of prominence in both his heart and mind. David understood the importance of following his Lord's leading and direction. Saul, on the other hand, acted out of his own devising and upon his own impulse.

Saul was given over to self-rule and self-sufficiency. He did not honor God as God. Saul's fear and insecurity compelled him to seek to destroy his God-anointed replacement. But the one he sought to destroy stood unwavering in his faith and his conviction that Saul was God's anointed. David was willing to wait on his God, and to trust Him implicitly.

Does your heart safely trust in your God and His promises? If not, He will soon bring you to that place as you continue to get to know Him by spending time with Him in your diligent study of His Word.

Israel

Judah

Every Man Dies...
But How?

Oh, the ignominious end of man who died because he didn't live for the Lord. Every man dies but not every man lives if he doesn't live for the Lord.

DAY ONE

Before you study the final chapter of 1 Samuel, you need to read the first nine chapters of 1 Chronicles. While these are not exciting chapters to read, still God considered them important enough to include in His Word. Therefore, we must also give them that place of respect. These nine chapters will actually give you a greater understanding of other Scriptures as you continue to study 2 Samuel, 1 Chronicles, and other portions of the Word. We'll take you through today's lesson one step at a time so that you don't get lost.

This segment of 1 Chronicles is primarily genealogical. To discover the scope of the genealogies, read 1:1 and 9:1,2. Note where Judah is carried in 9:1 and underline it as a geographical location. Then in 9:2 note where they are living.

It is important to remember that Chronicles was written after the return of the children of Israel from their 70 years of the Babylonian captivity to remind them of "the events or annals of the days, the years." Keep this date of writing in mind as you study these chapters.

Now read 1 Chronicles 1:1-4 and mark the following names in a distinctive way: *Adam, Noah,* and Noah's three sons: *Shem, Ham,* and *Japheth.* Remember we are looking at genealogies.

Next read verses 5-23 and again mark in a distinctive way the phrases, *the sons of Japheth, the sons of Ham,* and *the sons of Shem.* Then read Genesis 10:32 and note what you learn about these three men with respect to the inhabitants of this world.

Now read 1 Chronicles 1:24-34. Note who the main character is in this portion and note the names of his two sons. Mark them and note their genealogy. Do they descend from Shem, Ham, or Japheth?

In 1 Chronicles 1:34, note the names of Isaac's sons. In Genesis, Israel was named Jacob at his birth. God changed his name to Israel later.

Now read 1 Chronicles 2:1,2. Underline and number the sons of Israel. The chart THE BIRTH ORDER OF JACOB'S (ISRAEL'S) SONS on page 57 notes the birth order of these sons and their mother's names.

In 1 Chronicles 2:3-15, mark the phrase *the sons of Judah* and then look for and mark the name *David.* List David's genealogy from Judah through David's immediate father, Jesse, on your list about David in your notebook or put it in the margin of your Bible. Remember that the author of Chronicles gives the genealogy of Judah before the other sons of Israel. Why? What would be important to the exiles returning from Babylon to repossess their cities? The promises given to David. (You will want to keep this in mind as you study 1 Chronicles 10–19 in the next section of this book. All this parallels 2 Samuel 5–10. Study the chart HISTORICAL PARALLEL OF SAMUEL, KINGS, AND CHRONICLES on page 16.)

INSIGHT

The Birth Order of Jacob's (Israel's) Sons

Mother	Son
Leah	Reuben (born 1921 B.C.) Simeon Levi Judah
Bilhah (Rachel's maid)	Dan Naphtali
Zilpah (Leah's maid)	Gad Asher
Leah	Issachar Zebulun
Rachel	Joseph (born 1914 B.C.) Benjamin

Identify the themes of 1 Chronicles 1 and 2 and record these on the 1 CHRONICLES AT A GLANCE chart on page 63. As you record these themes, since you are covering genealogies in these chapters, you may simply want to title the chapters, *The Genealogies of* _____ and then fill in the main characters or tribes covered in these genealogies.

Day Two

Read 1 Chronicles 3:1-9. In verse 1, underline the phrase *the sons of David* and then underline the phrase *who were born to him in Hebron.*[22] In verse 5, underline *these were born to him in Jerusalem.*[23] List the names of David's sons in the margin of your Bible or on your list in your notebook.

Then read 1 Chronicles 3:10-16, which gives the line of kings who come from David through Solomon through Rehoboam. In verses 17-24, you see the list of the sons of Jeconiah. You will study him, along with the other kings, when you do *The International Inductive Study Series* on 1 and 2 Kings and 2 Chronicles.

Identify the theme of 1 Chronicles 3 and record it on the 1 CHRONICLES AT A GLANCE chart on page 63.

DAY THREE

Read 1 Chronicles 4–5 today. Every time you come across the mention of one of the 12 sons of Israel, mark it in a distinctive way. This list is also in 1 Chronicles 2:1,2.

In 1 Chronicles 5:1,2, note who Reuben's birthright is given to. Next to this verse, write "Joseph's sons: Manasseh and Ephraim." When you come to a mention of Manasseh or the half-tribe of Manasseh, mark it in a distinctive way. Manasseh is named twice. The tribe split when Canaan was divided. Half the tribe took the land east of the Jordan, and the other half west of the Jordan. Thus, the reference to the half-tribe of Manasseh. Don't forget to record your chapter themes on the 1 CHRONICLES AT A GLANCE chart.

DAY FOUR

Read 1 Chronicles 6–7. Underline who the sons of Levi were and number them in the text or write them in the margin of your Bible next to 1 Chronicles 6:1. Then mark in a distinctive way every introduction to a list of the sons of these three men, that is *the sons of Kohath,*[24] *the sons (of Gershom) [or Gershon], the sons of Merari.*[25]

It is interesting to note in 1 Chronicles 6:31 what some were appointed to do. Note also the contrast between 1 Chronicles 6:48 and 49.

Identify the themes of chapters 6 and 7 and record them on the 1 CHRONICLES AT A GLANCE chart on page 63.

DAY FIVE

Read 1 Chronicles 8. As you read this chapter, watch for the mention of Saul, his father, and his sons. Watch in particular for Jonathan and the name of his son, Merib-baal. Merib-baal is called Mephibosheth in 2 Samuel 4:4. This is something you will appreciate as you study 2 Samuel. Add any new insights to your lists on Saul and Jonathan in your notebook.

There are charts on the family trees of Saul and David on pages 70 and 71. When you look at the chart SAUL'S FAMILY TREE, you will see two individuals named Mephibosheth. Make sure you look at the one who was Jonathan's son and not the one who was Saul's son by his concubine.

Now read 1 Chronicles 9. Note why Judah (which consists of the tribes of Judah and Benjamin) was carried away into captivity and where it was taken. (The Northern Kingdom, made up of the other ten tribes, was taken into captivity by the Assyrians in 722 B.C.) As you read this chapter, watch for the gatekeepers and their assignments. It is also interesting to note verse 33 because it gives you insight into the place and priority of worship. You will also see a second account of Saul's genealogy in this chapter. If you glean any new insights on Saul, add them to your list.

Record the theme of chapters 8-9 on the 1 CHRONICLES AT A GLANCE chart.

DAY SIX

Today we return to the final chapter of 1 Samuel. Read
1 Chronicles 10 and then 1 Samuel 31. Mark the key words
Saul, Jonathan, and *David* and double underline geographical locations and mark time phrases as you did
before. Note the additional insights that are gleaned from
these two accounts of the same event. As you read these
accounts, remember the names of Saul's sons as given in 1
Chronicles 9:39. Compare them with those mentioned in 1
Chronicles 10:2. Note which son of Saul is not killed. Also
note the reason given in 1 Chronicles 10 for the death of
Saul. Add any new insights to your lists on Saul, Jonathan,
and David.

Record the chapter themes of 1 Samuel 31 and 1 Chronicles 10 on their respective AT A GLANCE charts. Then thank
the Lord for bringing you to this point of completion in your
study. You have hit a milestone, friend, and we commend
you. Are there any biblical principles that you could apply
to your life? If so, note any LFL and record it in the margin
of your Bible or in your notebook.

DAY SEVEN

Store in your heart: 1 Chronicles 10:13a or the entire
verse.

Read and discuss: 1 Samuel 31:1-13; 1 Chronicles 10:13,14.

QUESTIONS FOR DISCUSSION OR INDIVIDUAL STUDY

∾ Discuss the death of Saul. Cover the 5 W's and an H, getting all the facts down: who, what, when, where, why,

and how. What was the name of the son of Saul who survived?

∽ Discuss the life of Saul. What do you learn from the list you made on Saul? What do you learn from his life that you can apply to your own life or to the world and to the society in which you live?

∽ What is the most significant truth you learned in the study of 1 Samuel and 1 Chronicles 1–10?

THOUGHT FOR THE WEEK

Every man dies but not every man lives. Saul began well but he died in defeat, his head severed from his body, from his heart. It seems that with his rise to prominence he lost his fear of the One who allowed him to be king over Israel. He failed to keep the Word of God. He listened to the words of men and sought the counsel of a medium. Saul walked in partial obedience. Because of the way Saul lived, God had to look for another man to be king—one after His heart.

If you had lived then the way you are living now, would you have been another David? Would you have been a man or woman after God's own heart?

1 SAMUEL AT A GLANCE

Theme of 1 Samuel:

SEGMENT DIVISIONS

		MAIN DIVISIONS	CHAPTER THEMES	Author:
		SAMUEL, THE LAST JUDGE	1	
			2	Historical Setting:
			3	
			4	
			5	Purpose:
			6	
			7	
		FROM SAMUEL TO SAUL FROM JUDGES TO KINGS	8	Key Words:
			9	Samuel
			10	Saul
			11	covenant
			12	
			13	David
			14	King
			15	Spirit of the LORD
		THE PREPARATION OF ANOTHER KING	16	
			17	Achish
			18	
			19	Inquired of the LORD
			20	
			21	Jonathan
			22	evil spirit
			23	the ark of God (the ark of the covenant of the LORD, the ark of the covenant of God, the ark of the LORD)
			24	
			25	
			26	
			27	
			28	
			29	sin(s)
			30	evil things
			31	

1 Chronicles at a Glance

Theme of 1 Chronicles:

Segment Divisions

		Main Divisions	Chapter Themes	Author:
		The Genealogies of Israel	1	Historical Setting:
			2	
			3	
			4	Purpose:
			5	
			6	
			7	Key Words:
			8	Saul
			9	
		God Turns Kingdom to David	10	Jonathon
			11	David
			12	King
			13	
			14	
			15	
			16	
			17	
			18	
			19	
		David Builds Altar, Prepares for God's House	20	
			21	
			22	
			23	
			24	
			25	
			26	
			27	
			28	
			29	

SECOND SAMUEL

What Do You Do When the Bottom Falls Out?

Saul was dead. Ish-bosheth, the son of Saul was made king over all Israel. The men of Judah anointed David king over the house of Judah. A long war between the house of Saul and the house of David resulted. Assassinations took place. Israel killed her own sons.

A country once held together by God's rulership now split apart. David's enemies, from within Israel and from without, were hotly pursuing him. The situation wasn't good. The bottom was falling out. David was desperate.

Can you relate? Keeping your bearings when the bottom falls out is always difficult, isn't it? This week as you observe David's reactions, you can learn invaluable lessons on how to remain steady when the world seems to be shifting under you.

DAY ONE

As we begin our study of 2 Samuel, put yourself into context by reading 1 Samuel 30–31. As you read, watch where David is geographically at the close of chapter 30. Also note where Saul is when he dies. Consult the map THE DEATH OF SAUL AND HIS SONS on page 68. Then put this map into the greater context of the map on page 47, ISRAEL IN THE DAYS OF SAMUEL, SAUL, AND DAVID. When you finish, read 2 Samuel 1 and double underline any references to these same geographical locations. Marking pertinent geographical locations throughout this study will keep you in context.

Note David's proclamation regarding the mountains of Gilboa. (It is amazing to drive past those barren "mountains" in Israel today and see with your own eyes the fulfillment of David's words and to stand in the excavations of the theater at Beth-shan and look at the ancient tel [archeological mound] where Saul's body was nailed to the wall of the city.)

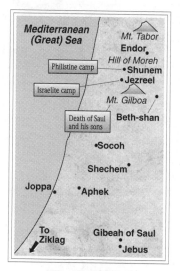

**The Death of
Saul and His Sons**

DAY TWO

Read 2 Samuel 1 again today. Then compare the account of Saul's death with the one given in 1 Samuel 31:1-6. As you read the account in 2 Samuel, note who brings the news of Saul's death to David, what this man is (verse 13), what he tells David about Saul's death, and why you think he is doing all this. List your insights on this man in your notebook. Then, keeping in mind that Scripture does not contradict Scripture, answer the question, "From whose perspective is 2 Samuel written?"

Be sure to notice how David responds to Saul's death as recorded in chapter 1. When you finish reading the chapter, review 1 Samuel 15:1-20 and watch for the various references to the Amalekites. By the way, when you study the book of Esther, you will discover that Haman, who sought to destroy the Jews, was an Amalekite.

Identify the theme of chapter 1 and record it on the 2 SAMUEL AT A GLANCE chart on page 113.

DAY THREE

You will use the same bookmark that you made in your study of 1 Samuel. Therefore, read 2 Samuel 2, marking the same key words you marked in 1 Samuel. Add *Abner, Joab,* and *Ish-bosheth* to your bookmark. Read 1 Chronicles 2:13-16 and note the relationship of Joab and his brothers to David. Record the insights you glean about each person on separate lists in your notebook. Ishbosheth is also called Eshbaal. You can see this on the chart SAUL'S FAMILY TREE on page 70. Refer to this chart for a better understanding of Saul's family. When you finish recording your insights, note all you learn about David from 2 Samuel 1 and 2.

As you read chapter 2, don't miss marking the phrase *David inquired of the LORD.*[1] Observe how David seeks God's direction for his every move and how God responds.

Remember to double underline geographical locations.
Time phrases are also important, so mark these with a clock
or as you did in 1 Samuel. From what you see in this passage,
can you understand one of the reasons Hebron is so important to Israel?

Don't forget to record the theme of this chapter on the
2 SAMUEL AT A GLANCE chart.

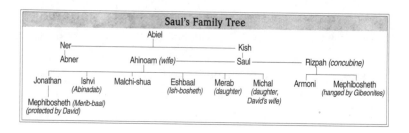

DAY FOUR

Read 2 Samuel 3 today. Mark the key words and add
to your lists any new insights you glean about the main
characters mentioned in this chapter. Include Abner's words
in 2 Samuel 3:9,10 on the list of insights about him. Note that
even David's enemies acknowledged him as having been
appointed king over Israel by the Lord. Record David's reactions to the events of chapter 3 on your list about him that
you began in 1 Samuel.

In 2 Samuel 3:2-5, there is a record of David's sons and
the names of their respective mothers. The chart DAVID'S
FAMILY TREE on page 71 will give you a visual picture of
David's lineage. It is helpful to keep this in mind as you
study about David's family.

Identify the theme of this chapter and record it on the
2 SAMUEL AT A GLANCE chart.

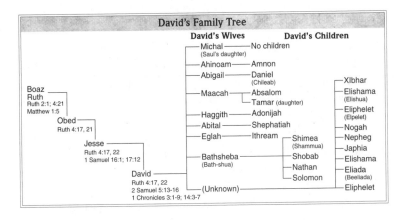

David's Family Tree

David's Wives	David's Children	
Michal (Saul's daughter)	No children	
Ahinoam	Amnon	
Abigail	Daniel (Chileab)	
Maacah	Absalom	
	Tamar (daughter)	
Haggith	Adonijah	
Abital	Shephatiah	
Eglah	Ithream	
Bathsheba (Bath-shua)	Shimea (Shammua)	
	Shobab	
	Nathan	
	Solomon	

David's Children (right column): Xlbhar, Elishama (Elishua), Eliphelet (Elpelet), Nogah, Nepheg, Japhia, Elishama, Eliada (Beeliada), Eliphelet

Boaz
Ruth
Ruth 2:1; 4:21
Matthew 1:5

Obed
Ruth 4:17, 21

Jesse
Ruth 4:17, 22
1 Samuel 16:1; 17:12

David
Ruth 4:17, 22
2 Samuel 5:13-16
1 Chronicles 3:1-9; 14:3-7

(Unknown)

DAY FIVE

Read 2 Samuel 4 to 5 today. Watch what you learn about the characters you have been following in your study. Record your observations on your lists. Mark key words, time phrases, and underline geographical references. Also begin a list on Mephibosheth. You will add to this later, so leave enough room for additional information.

As you read and mark 2 Samuel 4, notice how David responds to the killing of Ish-bosheth. Then from chapter 5 list everything you learn in respect to David becoming king.

Note those who anoint David king, the extent of his kingdom in relation to the various tribes, what David is to these people, and what David realizes with respect to all this. Also note the places he reigns and the time frame of these reigns.

Finally observe David's dependence upon the LORD for direction. Is there a lesson for your life (LFL) in all this? Record the themes of 2 Samuel 4 and 5.

DAY SIX

Today we need to go to 1 Chronicles 10:13–12:40. In this passage you will glean even more about this period in David's life. You will also see insights into David's mighty men and how they were drawn to him. Mark the same key words you have been marking in 1 and 2 Samuel. Watch for and mark any references to time and to geographical locations. Notice what Jerusalem is called in 1 Chronicles and note too the name given to the people who lived in that area.

Don't forget to add to your list on David any new insights you glean about him.

Identify the themes of 1 Chronicles 10, 11, and 12 and record them on the 1 CHRONICLES AT A GLANCE chart.

DAY SEVEN

Store in your heart: 2 Samuel 5:10.
Read and Discuss: 1 Samuel 31:1-6; 2 Samuel 1–5.

QUESTIONS FOR DISCUSSION OR INDIVIDUAL STUDY

∾ Why was David mourning the death of Saul? David loved Jonathan like a brother, but how did he feel about Saul?

∾ What was David's reaction after hearing of the death of Saul and Jonathan? Compare David's reaction to Saul's actions toward him in the past.

∾ What was David's response to the Amalekite? Why did he respond in this way?

∾ Compare the story of the Amalekite to the account given in 1 Samuel 31:1-6. What motive might the Amalekite have had for telling David that he had killed Saul (2 Samuel 1:5-11)? What had David returned from doing in 2 Samuel 1:1?

∾ Discuss what you learn about David in relation to Abner's death. What do you learn about the attitude of David's heart (2 Samuel 3:31-39)?

∾ Discuss what you learned about David's rise to kingship. Discuss the various stages, how he comes to rule over all 12 tribes, and God's part in all this. What do you learn about God from David's life? How can you apply this to your own life?

∾ Second Samuel 5:17-25 mentions two battles with the Philistines. Compare God's instructions and David's actions in each of these battles.

∾ What is clear about David's relationship with the Lord in 2 Samuel 5:17-25? Where does David go in his time of need? What about you? Do you seek the Lord's wisdom on a consistent basis for the decisions you make in your life?

∾ Discuss your insights about David from the first five chapters of 2 Samuel.

Thought for the Week

David's rival, King Saul, is put to death. The opposing general is also killed. The armies who have warred against David now join forces with him and pledge their allegiance to him. Yet David never celebrates the news of his enemies deaths or lords his position over the men who have become a part of his forces. Instead, he mourns, weeps, and fasts. David keeps his focus on God, not on his own circumstances— whether they bring defeat or victory. David fully grasped God's sovereignty—that God is in control of the circumstances of life. David understood that the glory belonged to God.

During a crisis, is God's rulership (sovereignty) over your circumstances uppermost in your thoughts? Do you continually seek His direction? Can you, do you, trust Him to guide you? Are you willing to submit to His leadership even when it takes an unexpected turn or when it isn't the response you wanted or the direction you had hoped to go in? Or, at that point, do you compromise and work your own plan into His?

What did you learn from David's life? Remember, Beloved, that the things written beforehand were written for our encouragement. Walk in the light of what you are learning about David's God...and yours.

Listen to what He says to you. He can be trusted, and you can be changed.

What Happens When You Don't Seek God His Way?

As you do this week's study, you'll see how we need to make sure that in our enthusiasm to serve God we do it His way ... not our way.

DAY ONE

Second Samuel 6 is a very interesting and significant chapter that centers on the ark of the covenant. Therefore, mark every reference to *the ark (the ark of God, the ark of the LORD, the ark of the covenant of God)* in the same way you marked these in 1 Samuel. Remember to mark pronouns that refer to His ark. Also mark all references to time and note any geographical locations. Record any new insights you discover about the ark. Then, when you finish this chapter, read the account of the same event in 1 Chronicles 13 and mark *the ark of our God.*

When you finish reading 1 Chronicles 13, look at Numbers 4:4-16. You might want to record this cross-reference. Identify the theme of these chapters and record them on the appropriate AT A GLANCE charts.

DAY TWO

Our focus today will be 1 Chronicles 14–15. As you read chapter 14 and mark the key words from your bookmark, watch what finally occurs to David—what he realizes in this chapter. Note how his reputation spreads, who is behind it all, and why.

Then read chapter 15 and mark the key words. Once again give careful attention to what you learn about the ark and about what David has learned with respect to moving the ark. Add to your list on the ark what you observe in this chapter. Mark *the ark of the Lord God of Israel*[2] and *the ark of the covenant of the LORD* as you have marked other references to the ark previously.

Do you remember reading yesterday how David's wife, Michal, responded to David's dancing before the ark? Compare what you learned yesterday and today with 1 Samuel 18:20,21. This passage might help explain why Michal reacted to David as she did. Note the consequences of her behavior as recorded in the 2 Samuel account.

Record any new insights you glean about David on the running list you are keeping on him.

Finally don't forget to record the chapter themes for these two chapters on the AT A GLANCE chart for 1 Chronicles.

DAY THREE

We want to turn our attention to 1 Chronicles 16. This is a marvelous chapter for broadening our understanding of worship. Read it thoughtfully, marking the key words and giving special attention to who does what. Add any new insights to your list on the ark.

The word *covenant* is a very important word in this passage. Since this is a key word, you should have marked it and its pronouns already. However, make sure that you distinguish it from references to the ark of the covenant of God.

Note what you learn about God and His commitment to His covenants in this chapter.

Remember when you read those very long and laborious chapters at the beginning of 1 Chronicles? Now is the time to reap some of the benefits of your diligence. Next to 1 Chronicles 16:41, write 1 Chronicles 6:31-39 as a cross-reference and then read this passage again. What do you learn about the importance of praise and thanksgiving?

Record the theme of this chapter on the 1 CHRONICLES AT A GLANCE chart.

DAY FOUR

Read 2 Samuel 7 and 1 Chronicles 17. In these chapters, you will meet an important person, Nathan. You will want to make a list in your notebook of the things you learn about him.

As you read, mark the key words and time phrases (including the word *forever*). Also mark the word *establish*[3]*(ed)*[4] in 2 Samuel 7 and 1 Chronicles 17 and add the word *house* to your bookmark. However, only mark the word *house* if it refers to the "house of God"—*not* to the "house (family) of David." Add any new insights about the ark and about David to the list in your notebook. Note both David's sense of awe at God's word through Nathan the prophet and how he responds to what Nathan tells him. Record too what God says concerning David's descendants in 2 Samuel 7:12-16 and what you learn about David's heart toward God in 2 Samuel 7:18-29.

DAY FIVE

As you read 2 Samuel 8, what phrase concerning God is repeated in verses 6 and 14? Does this help you to understand why David prospered? Note your insights on David. Also mark any key words from your bookmark.

Now read 1 Chronicles 18 for additional insights and mark the same key words.

Identify the chapter themes and record these on the AT A GLANCE charts.

DAY SIX

Read 2 Samuel 9, which is certainly a most enlightening and interesting chapter. Once again you will come across Mephibosheth. Carefully observe all you learn about him and add it to the list you began on him when you read 2 Samuel 4:4. Mark these as cross-references in the margin of your Bible as you have done before. Then, to refresh your memory, read again about the covenant between Jonathan and David in 1 Samuel 20:14-17,42. You should get a sense of the gravity of making a covenant and remaining true to a covenant. Mark any key words and add to your lists.

Identify the theme of 2 Samuel 9 and record it on the 2 SAMUEL AT A GLANCE chart.

DAY SEVEN

Store in your heart: 1 Chronicles 15:13b.
Read and discuss: Numbers 4:4-16; 1 Chronicles 13; 15:25-29; 2 Samuel 7:12-17; 2 Samuel 9.

QUESTIONS FOR DISCUSSION OR INDIVIDUAL STUDY

1 Chronicles 13; 15:25-29

∾ Where had the ark of the covenant been before David decided to move it? How long had it been there? What prompted David to move it?

∾ Discuss what happened when they brought the ark from Kiriath-jearim.

∾ Why did God kill Uzza? How did David respond?

∾ What does this tell you about God? Make sure you discuss Numbers 4:4-16.

∾ Do such insights have any impact or effect on your relationship to God?

∾ Where does the ark end up? How does it get there?

∾ What do you learn about God from the thanksgiving rendered Him by Asaph and his relatives? Why Asaph and his relatives?

2 Samuel 7:12-17

∾ What was David's desire? Would it be accomplished? How?

∾ What promises did God give David regarding the house of David—the future of his descendants?

2 Samuel 9

∾ Who was Mephibosheth?

∾ What happened to him when he was a child? Why?

∾ Why was David so kind to Mephibosheth? What did David do for him?

∾ What does this account teach you about the cutting of a covenant?

∾ How did God speak to your heart personally this week? What impact, if any, has this lesson had on your understanding of or relationship to God? Will it alter the way you think or behave? Why or why not? How?

THOUGHT FOR THE WEEK

At every turn of the page in your study this week you have seen in various life situations the gravity, the import, of taking God at His Word. There is a verse of Scripture that says that God watches over His Word to perform it. We have seen how true this is.

No matter how much time has elapsed since God gave His commandments, His instructions, the revelation of His heart, or His desire in various matters, we have ample evidence that He expects us to "seek Him according to the ordinance" (1 Chronicles 15:13). We are not to choose our way above His way. No matter how noble our intentions, even as David's were noble in restoring the ark of the covenant to its proper status in the life of the nation, what we do must be done God's way. God is a holy God, and when we do not comply with His way we are not treating Him as holy.

Although David failed to move the ark according to God's specific instructions and reaped the consequences, we see him honoring his covenant with Jonathan in extending loving-kindness to Jonathan's son, Mephibosheth.

Weren't we just like Mephibosheth before we were saved—running, hiding, living in fear in a barren place because we were ignorant of a covenant made on our behalf? A covenant of grace that grants us the right to live with the King of kings, to dine at His table forever, to be "served" by the Spirit of God who makes us know our inheritance because of the covenant—even though we all are lame, so to speak, in both feet.

"Come and dine," the Master calls. "Come and dine." You can feast at Jesus' table anytime...even though you became lame in both feet as you ran from Him in your sin!

You can feast because a new covenant has been cut for you in the death, burial, and resurrection of Jesus Christ. The Spirit of God has been given to you and you have been made an heir of God, a joint-heir with Jesus Christ. Now, dear friend, order your life accordingly.

What Happens When Sin Goes Unchecked?

In our day of moral relativism, most people believe that as long as they don't force their lifestyle on others, their own behavior is a matter of personal choice. Should others be concerned about the way you live? Is it anyone's business what you do privately? Or do the consequences of disobedience, sin, and rebellion affect the lives of others around you? If so, how deep and far-reaching are they? How long can a consequence endure?

This week we will examine the all-too-human aspects of David's life ... and hopefully learn lessons for our own lives.

DAY ONE

Read 2 Samuel 10 and 1 Chronicles 19. You will see an interesting account which shows the gravity of listening to the unwarranted, unfounded suspicions of others. Mark pertinent key words, time phrases, and locations. Also add to your list on David and record your theme for each chapter on its respective AT A GLANCE chart.

As you read the Word of God, you will often find admonitions—exhortations to be strong and courageous. Read 2 Samuel 10:12 and then find and mark the parallel verse in 1 Chronicles 19. What is a lesson for life in these verses? You may want to record this in the margin of your Bible or highlight the verse. Then read Joshua 1:6-9 and see where courage comes from.

Be strong and courageous, dear friend.

DAY TWO

Read 2 Samuel 11 and mark key words. Also mark every reference to *Uriah*. When you finish, list in your notebook everything you learn about Uriah. Then contrast David's behavior with Uriah's. Record your observations about David on the list in your notebook. As you do, note what happened when David tried to cover his sin rather than confess and forsake it. Read Proverbs 28:13.

Identify the theme of this chapter and record it on the 2 SAMUEL AT A GLANCE chart.

DAY THREE

Read 2 Samuel 11:26–12:31. Carefully observe the main characters in this passage and what role each plays in the series of events that follow. As you read, give careful attention to all the Lord does in this chapter. In doing so, you will see the heart and ways of God with respect to the disobedient behavior of those who belong to Him.

Mark the key words from your bookmark and all the references to *Nathan* and the phrase *David therefore inquired of God*.[5]

Add to your lists on David and Nathan. Be sure to record the consequences of David's sin, especially how he responded when he was confronted (verses 13,14).

In this chapter, we are introduced to *Solomon*. Begin a list on Solomon, and make sure you note the name given to him by God.

By the way, have you considered that when you sin, God's enemies are given the opportunity to blaspheme Him?

Identify the theme of chapter 12 and record it on the 2 SAMUEL AT A GLANCE chart.

DAY FOUR

Read 2 Samuel 13. Mark the key words and all references to *Tamar, Amnon,* and *Absalom.* Record the time references and follow the sequence of events. Make a list of what you learn from observing Tamar and Amnon. Note Amnon's problem and how it was handled. As you read, watch for the change that occurs in Amnon in verse 15. Observe that Amnon's sin with Tamar began with deception (13:5,6).

Also begin a list of insights on Absalom. How long was he willing to wait before he avenged his sister (verse 23)? What were the consequences of his actions (2 Samuel 13:37-39)?

Identify the theme of this chapter and record it on the 2 SAMUEL AT A GLANCE chart.

DAY FIVE

Read 2 Samuel 14. This chapter has many valuable insights on relationships—look for them and think about them. There is much to learn as you observe the lives and reactions of the people mentioned in this chapter. Watch for lessons for life (LFL), which you can record in the margin of your Bible.

Mark key words from your bookmark. Note what you learn about David and Absalom on the lists in your notebook. Also after you mark the references to *Joab,* make a list of what you learn about him and carefully observe the role he plays in Absalom's return. Underline the geographical locations, mark the time phrases, and note the sequence of events.

Identify the theme of this chapter and record it on the 2 SAMUEL AT A GLANCE chart.

DAY SIX

Read 2 Samuel 15. Add *Ahithophel* to your bookmark and begin a list on what you learn about him. Mark the references to *the ark of the covenant of God (the ark of God)* and add your insights to your list on David. Mark other key words from your bookmark and continue adding to your lists.

Did you see a change in Absalom as you read chapter 15? Record your insights on Absalom in your notebook. Also list what you learn from observing David's response to these events. Note his brokenness and submission before God. Finally, carefully observe David's prayer in 2 Samuel 15:31 and then, as you read next week's lesson, observe how God answers this prayer.

Identify the theme of this chapter and record it on the 2 SAMUEL AT A GLANCE chart.

DAY SEVEN

Store in your heart: Proverbs 28:13.
Read and discuss: Genesis 3:1-7; 2 Samuel 11–15.

QUESTIONS FOR DISCUSSION OR INDIVIDUAL STUDY

∾ Discuss the circumstances surrounding David's sins related to Bathsheba and Uriah and the sequence of events involved in both instances. What should David have been doing (2 Samuel 11:1)? Read the record of original sin in Genesis 3:1-7. Note the progression of Eve's actions that led to her ultimate act of disobedience. Do you see any parallels between Genesis 3 and this account of David's sins?

∾ How did David's first sin lead to the next sin and the next? Discuss the sequence of these sins and the way they came about. What do you learn from this example that you can apply to your life today?

∾ What motivated Nathan to confront David (2 Samuel 12:1)? How did Nathan approach David? What can you learn about confronting leaders who have sinned?

∾ When did David confess his sins?

∾ What were the consequences of his sin(s)? Discuss the immediate and later consequences that are recorded in 2 Samuel 13-15.

∾ How was God's graciousness expressed to David?

∾ Discuss other characteristics in David's life that you observed this week as you looked at his dealings with Absalom.

∾ Discuss the effect sin has on the sinner and how it impacts the lives of others.

∾ Discuss the way our society deals with sin today. Where do you think it will lead? How do you think God will respond and why? Does He seem to be responding now or ignoring or overlooking our sin? Has God changed with respect to sin?

∾ How do you deal with sin in your own life? Are you prone to cover your sin? Why?

ᙎ Discuss what you see in David's life by the turn of events in 2 Samuel 15. What do you see in this man in 15:25,26? Would you trust God this much?

ᙎ What have you personally learned this week?

THOUGHT FOR THE WEEK

David was a man of discipline, dedication, and determination, a man chosen and anointed by God to reign over His chosen people. His commitment to God's calling was evidenced in the way he lived.

As you compiled your insights on David, you saw his humility—awed that God had chosen him, submitting to His will and dealings with him, inquiring of God, seeking and obeying His counsel, honoring Saul, waiting on God . . . trusting God. David was a leader faithful to his God, a diligent shepherd of His people.

Then one spring while his army went to battle, David the valiant warrior chose to stay behind. That seemingly insignificant compromise left David in a vulnerable position. When temptation reared its head, David did not bridle his emotions or submit his desires to the purposes of the God he loved and served. Rather, he gave in to the desires of his flesh. And although cognizant of his sin, aware of the forgiveness and mercy of God, David continued in his downward course on a slippery slope that would take him farther than he ever intended to go—a course that would cost him more than he ever dreamed. Sin is that way. Its pleasures only last for a season.

Is God intervening right now? Calling you, friend, to accountability even as He called David to account through the prophet Nathan? As Nathan was sent by God to confront David, leaving no room for denial but exposing the ugliness of his sins and the consequences of his behavior, has God used this week's study to do the same thing in your life?

How will you respond? Will it be as David responded— not excusing himself, nor blaming others, but confessing and taking responsibility for his actions? David was brought face-to-face with the truth about his own behavior. Instead of excusing himself or blaming others, David confessed and fully repented. And although the consequences came, David was not embittered. He bore them like a man . . . a man whose heart was God's, a man who so trusted in his God that he could say, "Let Him do to me as seems good to Him."

It is one thing to sin . . . it is another to not concur with God that sin is sin and that it is worthy of His judgment. And it is yet another not to believe God when you hear "the LORD also has taken away your sin." If your heart is God's, your response will be like David's as recorded in Psalm 51. You will acknowledge that ultimately it is God against whom you have sinned and that only He can forgive and restore to you the joy of your salvation.

Remember that "the sacrifices of God are a broken spirit; a broken and a contrite heart, O God, Thou wilt not despise" (Psalm 51:17). Remember that it is never too late to respond to the many ways God reaches out to draw you in. God will forgive and cleanse, no matter what you have done. Spend time alone with God, asking Him to reveal any places of vulnerability in you that exist because in some area you have not wholeheartedly followed. Then be obedient to what He tells you.

WEEK FOUR

Is There Security in God, Even When All the Human Odds Are Stacked Against You?

Civil war. Armies with giants. The curses of men. Betrayal by family and friends. This week has it all! Read on, friend, to see how a child of God can survive such trauma.

DAY ONE

As you read 2 Samuel 16 and mark the key words, you are going to read more about Mephibosheth and his servant Ziba. To refresh your memory about Mephibosheth, go back to your notes in your notebook or read 2 Samuel 4:4; 9. As you read this week, you will see that there is more to this situation than meets the eye.

Watch Ahithophel's advice to Absalom. Also take special note of what happens with Shimei, as you will also meet him again this week.

Observe David's trust in the fact that his circumstances are controlled by the Lord (16:5-13). Compare 2 Samuel 16:20-23 with 2 Samuel 12:11. You might want to mark these as cross-references in the margin of your Bible.

Identify the theme of this chapter and record it on the 2 SAMUEL AT A GLANCE chart.

DAY TWO

As you read and mark 2 Samuel 17, don't miss the sovereignty of God overruling the counsel of man. In fact you may want to mark every reference to *counsel* or *advice* in this chapter. Add to your lists on David, Absalom, and Ahithophel.

Note the difference between David's attitude toward killing Saul the king (1 Samuel 24:6; 26:9-11) and Absalom's attitude toward killing David the king in chapter 17.

Remember to record the chapter theme.

DAY THREE

Read 2 Samuel 18. Mark your key words and add to your lists. When you finish 1 and 2 Samuel you are going to have some very valuable notes on these people who are part of Israel's history, and with those notes you will have a wealth of insights into how a man's relationship with the Lord and his fellowman shapes his character and the outcome of his life.

As you read verse 33, rehearse David's relationship with Absalom. What would have happened had David restored his son to full fellowship after he slew Amnon for violating Tamar? Although we will never know, it is worth considering with respect to our relationships with others who have failed in one way or another.

Record your chapter theme for 2 Samuel 18 on the 2 SAMUEL AT A GLANCE chart.

DAY FOUR

We are going to divide your reading assignment on 2 Samuel 19, so read only verses 1-23 today. Watch for and mark any form of the phrase *bring back the king*.[6]

As you come to 2 Samuel 19:16-23, remember that you first met Shimei in 2 Samuel 16:5-13. Note how Shimei responds to David now that he is accepted as king. It will be interesting to see what happens to Shimei when you study 1 and 2 Kings and 2 Chronicles. How we urge you to begin that study as soon as you finish this one. If you desire to know God's heart, you must continue in His Word, and 1 and 2 Kings is a natural next step since it is merely a continuation of your current study.

DAY FIVE

Finish observing and marking 2 Samuel 19:24-43 today. Compare this account about Mephibosheth with what Ziba said in 2 Samuel 16:1-4. What seems to be the truth and why? What do you learn from this passage about listening to the reports of others?

Record the theme of 2 Samuel 19 on your AT A GLANCE chart.

DAY SIX

David's troubles are still not over. Read 2 Samuel 20 and meet Sheba and observe how one man can turn a mob, a crowd—ten tribes to be exact—around. And see too how the wise counsel of a woman can spare a city. Mark key words and then record the chapter theme.

DAY SEVEN

Store in your heart: 2 Samuel 16:12.

Read and discuss: 2 Samuel 16:1-14; 19:16-30; 15:31; 16:20-24; 18:33–19:13.

QUESTIONS FOR DISCUSSION OR INDIVIDUAL STUDY

2 Samuel 16:1-14; 19:16-30

~ Discuss all you learned from 2 Samuel about Mephibosheth in the light of the 5 W's and an H. Discuss the
loyalty or lack of loyalty of Mephibosheth, taking into
account what David did for him and why, what Ziba
reported and possibly why, Mephibosheth's condition
when he encountered David, and his response to David.
What lessons are to be learned from these accounts that
you can apply to your own life?

~ Discuss what you learn from Shimei's response to David
and David's response to him . . . or was it to God? What
do you learn from these incidents?

2 Samuel 15:31; 16:20-24

~ What did David pray regarding the counsel of Ahithophel? Was the counsel of Ahithophel foolishness? How
did God answer David's prayer?

~ Did David do anything to participate in the answering of
this prayer? How does this strike you? Was David chas-
tised for it? What do you learn from this account?

~ What do you learn from all this that you can apply to
your life?

2 Samuel 18:33–19:13

~ How did Absalom die? Do you think this was simply a
twist of fate that held him by the hair?

~ What did you learn from observing Absalom's life? What
did you learn from David's response to his son and his
reaction to his death? What did David seem to want?

∾ Discuss Joab's words to David with respect to his mourning over the death of his son. What is David's response to Joab? Discuss 2 Samuel 19:13.

∾ What did you learn from marking the phrase *bring back the king?*

∾ Did God show favor to David? Did He look on David's affliction and return good to him instead of cursing him?

∾ What have you learned from these chapters which you can apply to your own life? Discuss what you have learned about God . . . and about the proper response of man in the day of his adversity.

THOUGHT FOR THE WEEK

David was a man who desired the heart of God, and although he was not perfect, God was still there for him in the day of his adversity. And David knew it. So when his son betrayed him, when his own people rose up against him and were torn in a civil war centered on him, when he was publicly cursed and then allegedly betrayed by one whom he had shown mercy because of a covenant, David knew where his deliverance would come from. "Perhaps the LORD will look on my affliction and return good to me instead of his [Shimei's] cursing this day" (2 Samuel 16:12).

Dear friend, beloved of God, do you walk with the same confidence? Surely as you have studied David's life you have seen how God moves on behalf of those whose hearts are fully His, even though they stumble over their feet of clay.

While we don't know what is transpiring in your life right now, we do know that if it is unrelenting sorrow and pain, the God of David is right there . . . able to show Himself strong on your behalf. So walk to the beat of His heart, in the light of His counsel. Remember God is sovereign and He can, with the breath of His omnipotence, change the course of events whenever it is best for you . . . and for His glory.

When God Calls into Account the Covenants of Man

As you study this week, you will see the solemnity of keeping a covenant made in the presence of a covenant-keeping God—and it will bring assurance of the faithfulness of the God who watches over His Word to perform it.

DAY ONE

Read 2 Samuel 21:1-14 very carefully. There are important lessons in this passage about the solemnity of making a covenant with another and keeping it. Mark the key words, time phrases, and geographical locations, then cross-reference this passage with Joshua 9. You will learn more about the covenant made by Israel with the Gibeonites in Joshua 9. There is no biblical account of Saul's violation of this covenant, except for its mention in this account. However, we know it occurred because of this passage. As you study what David does to stop the famine, you will find it helpful to consult the chart, SAUL'S FAMILY TREE on page 70.

Add new observations to your lists on David and Mephibosheth. Note how David honors his covenant (1 Samuel 20:12-23,42) with Jonathan regarding his descendants.

DAY TWO

Read 2 Samuel 21:15-22 and then read 1 Chronicles 20:1-3, which parallels 2 Samuel 12:26-31 that we have already studied. Mark your key words in 2 Samuel 21:15-22 and 1 Chronicles 20:4-8. Then identify the themes of these chapters and record them on the appropriate AT A GLANCE charts.

DAY THREE

We will spend the next three days looking at an incredible chapter—2 Samuel 22. It is filled with awesome insights into God and what it means to have Him as your God. We want you to look at this chapter in bite-sized pieces so you will have adequate time to meditate on its wonderful precepts of life.

Read verse 1 for the occasion of this song and then read the first 18 verses. List in your notebook what David does and how God responds. Noting these insights will minister to your heart. When you finish, talk to God about what you have learned about Him. Ask Him to show you how these truths have been realized in your life . . . and then spend some time worshiping and thanking Him for who He is.

Record any LFL in the margin of your Bible.

DAY FOUR

Today read 2 Samuel 22:19-31, following the same format as yesterday. Mark every reference to *righteousness* or *cleanness*. Also mark every occurrence of *blameless*[7] in a distinctive way or color.

DAY FIVE

Finish reading 2 Samuel 22:32-51 again, following the last two days' instructions. Be sure to give yourself time for meditation, praise, and worship as you realize that 2 Samuel 22:2-51 is Psalm 18! Don't miss marking *blameless*[8] in verse 33. Then identify the theme of this chapter and record it on the 2 SAMUEL AT A GLANCE chart.

DAY SIX

Your assignment for today is 2 Samuel 23. As you read verse one, note how David describes himself and what his last words are. Also note how 2 Samuel 23:1,2 *prove* Davidic psalms are divinely inspired! Then as you go through the account of David's mighty men, you may want to underline the name of each of them. There are some interesting tales of the exploits of these valiant men which we believe you will enjoy. You will also want to note who it is that brings about the victory. The account of these men is also in 1 Chronicles 11, which you have already studied. (Remember Chronicles was written after the return from captivity to give the children of Israel encouragement as they returned to their land. First and 2 Samuel and 1 and 2 Kings were written before they went into captivity. Thus, the material in Chronicles is laid out differently.)

Mark key words and add to your list any new insights on David. Identify the theme of chapter 23 and record it on the 2 SAMUEL AT A GLANCE chart.

DAY SEVEN

Store in your heart: 2 Samuel 22:29 or 32,33.
   Read and discuss: 2 Samuel 21; Joshua 9:1-27; 2 Samuel 12:13; 23:20-33.

QUESTIONS FOR DISCUSSION OR INDIVIDUAL STUDY

2 Samuel 21:1-14; Joshua 9:1-27

∾ According to 2 Samuel 21, what consequences do David and the nation of Israel suffer as a result of sin?

∾ What do you learn about the gravity of the covenant made with the Gibeonites? You might want to review Joshua 9:1-27.

∾ Whose sin caused these consequences?

∾ What did David have to do in order to save Israel from famine?

∾ Why did David spare Mephibosheth?

∾ What have you learned about the gravity of entering into a covenant? What does this tell you about being in covenant with God?

2 Samuel 23:20-33; 12:13

∾ In this passage David describes himself as blameless. He says he has kept the ways of the Lord, kept himself from iniquity. He talks of his cleanness before God. How can David say these things about himself when he sinned with Bathsheba and in essence ordered the death of Bathsheba's husband, Uriah?

∾ Read 2 Samuel 12:13. What does this tell you about David's understanding and acceptance of the forgiveness of God?

∾ How do you deal with your sins ... your failure to walk in righteousness? Could you say the same thing David is saying in these verses? Why? On what basis?

ᴥ If you have confessed and forsaken your sins and you cannot say what David says, are you believing God? If not, what does this say regarding your understanding of God or your faith in His Word?

ᴥ What other insights blessed you as you meditated on 2 Samuel 23?

THOUGHT FOR THE WEEK

It is a solemn thing to be in covenant with God. As you have seen this week, God watches over covenants made by men and calls them into account. Of course, this is what Jonathan asked for when he made the covenant with David and said, "May the LORD require *it* at the hands of David's enemies" (1 Samuel 20:16).

If God watches over the covenants of men, how much more will He watch over the ones He makes. This, Beloved, is why you can be assured of forgiveness when you ask for it. This is what the new covenant is all about—"this is the covenant which I will make...for I will forgive their iniquity, and their sin I will remember no more" (Jeremiah 31:33,34). This then, friend, is why you, with David, can say you are blameless before God.

So remember that God is your strong fortress and that He sets the blameless in His way and presses you on toward the high calling of the covenant cut for you in the blood of His only begotten Son.

Be Strong and Courageous...
He's Your Rock, Your Fortress

Have you ever wondered if it's really worth it to live differently than the world? To live in obedience to God? As you will see again this week, the life of David bears adequate testimony of the consequences of disobedience and the blessings of obedience.

Day One

Read 2 Samuel 24. As you mark key words, geographical locations, and time phrases, also mark any reference to *the angel of the Lord (the angel)* in a distinctive way or color. Remember to mark the references to *sinned⁹ (iniquity)*.

We would also encourage you to number in the text the three choices David was given in verse 13. As you record your insights, note David's last actions—his response when he recognized his sin (24:10). Also note why he chose the judgment he did (2 Samuel 24:14).

When you identify the theme of this chapter and record it on the 2 SAMUEL AT A GLANCE chart, you will have a complete record of the main themes of each chapter in this book. Congratulations. If you have an *International*

Inductive Study Bible, you will want to record these on the AT A GLANCE chart at the end of 2 Samuel.

Day Two

Having completed 2 Samuel, it is now time to finish 1 Chronicles, which you will do in the remainder of this week's study. Your assignment for today is to read 1 Chronicles 21 to gain even greater insights into the events you read about yesterday.

Mark the same key words you marked yesterday.[10] Give special attention to time phrases and geographical locations. Also note that Araunah, who owned the threshing floor bought by David, is also called Ornan. Ornan was a Jebusite.

As you read this chapter, you are going to learn much more about the angel of the Lord. Therefore, you might find it helpful to list your insights in your notebook.

As you come to verse 28, read through 1 Chronicles 22:2. Note where the tabernacle of the Lord was at that time and where the house of the Lord would be built. The threshing floor of Ornan is on the temple mount in Jerusalem where the Dome of the Rock and the El Aqsa Mosque now stand. Look at 2 Chronicles 3:1. You might want to write this cross-reference in your Bible next to an appropriate place in 1 Chronicles 21 and 2 Samuel 24.

Knowing all this makes the news from Israel more relevant, doesn't it?

Record your theme for 1 Chronicles 21 on the 1 CHRONICLES AT A GLANCE chart.

Day Three

Read 1 Chronicles 22–23. As you mark your key words, give special attention to what you learn with respect to the house of God. Note who is to build it, why they are to build it, who provides for its building, what it will be like, where it will be located, and what God says about it. Observe David's commands to the leaders of Israel.

Doing a thorough study of all this will give you great insight into the controversies occurring in the city of Jerusalem—over the city itself and over the temple mount area. Pay careful attention to 1 Chronicles 23:25. Note how God is described in this verse and where He dwells forever.

On the 1 CHRONICLES AT A GLANCE chart, record your themes for these chapters.

DAY FOUR

Although your reading assignment for today will be insightful, it may become a little wearisome. However, it is necessary if you are going to know the content of 1 Chronicles.

Remember Chronicles is an account of "the events, or annals of the days, the years" as you will see in this section when you will read about the duties and numbers of the various men assigned to these tasks. All this was recorded after the captivity as a strong admonition to the children of Israel not to forsake again the temple and the proper worship of their holy God. These facts become a great source of information to Israel as her people will someday rebuild the temple and worship in it again.

As you read chapters 24–27, look for the key verses in each chapter that give you an explanation of the broader content of the chapter. As you read chapters 24—27, you will notice that the information centers on the descendants of Aaron and the tribe of Levi. So watch for key verses like 24:1-7,19; 25:1-8, and so on.

Mark key words . . . especially watching the references to *the house of the LORD*[11] *(the house of God)*. What do you learn about *the house of the LORD?* You may want to list these in your notebook.

When you finish your assignment, congratulate yourself for your diligence and then record the chapter themes of these four chapters on the AT A GLANCE chart.

DAY FIVE

As you read and mark 1 Chronicles 28 today, make sure you read it slowly enough and thoroughly enough that you don't miss all that is being said about and to Solomon. There are wonderful lessons for life in this chapter . . . admonitions that parents should give to their children.

Mark the key words and then take careful notes on Solomon and David. Note how David knew what to instruct Solomon with respect to the house of the LORD and all its vessels.

Record the theme of the chapter.

DAY SIX

Well, friend, we have come to the final chapter of 1 Chronicles. You have persevered well and are to be commended. We know that if you live in the light of what you have learned you will truly be a mighty man, mighty woman of God. Our prayer for you is in verse 19, "and give to [you] a perfect heart to keep Thy commandments, Thy testimonies, and Thy statutes, and to do *them* all . . ." The temple being built today is the one mentioned in Ephesians 2:19-22 as you are faithful in your calling to proclaim the glorious gospel of our Lord Jesus Christ.

Our question is, "Are you sure, without a shadow of a doubt, that you are part of that temple?" If not, then you must repent—have a change of mind regarding who God is and who Jesus Christ is—and respond accordingly. God is your Creator, and you were made for His pleasure. Therefore, you are to live for Him, not for yourself.

To live for yourself is to walk your own way, and that is sin. You were born in sin, you live in sin, and consequently you are a slave to sin. But Jesus Christ, who is one with God, having the same character and attributes, left heaven to become a man.

Jesus was born of a virgin by the name of Mary in order to become flesh and blood, like you, so that He could die in your place. He paid the price for your sin, death. That death is not only physical death, but spiritual death, which separates you from God forever in a place He prepared for the devil and his angels—the lake of fire. The lake of fire is called the second death, as you will see when you do *The IISS* on Revelation, *Behold, Jesus Is Coming!*

But God, who was not willing that any perish in this eternal lake of fire, loved you so much that He crucified His Son for you, placing all your sins and all the sins of mankind on Jesus, who never sinned. Because Jesus was without sin, death and the grave could not hold Him. However, because God's holy righteousness was satisfied by Jesus' sacrifice, He raised Jesus from the dead, guaranteeing that all who repent and believe in the Lord Jesus Christ will have forgiveness of sins and the gift of eternal life.

To believe means "to put your trust in what God says about His Son"—His person, His work, His promises. Jesus is the only way to God. There is no other way. He is life—apart from Him there is no life. He is the truth—He cannot lie and will not lie. He is to be believed, and He said that He came that you might have life and have it abundantly. Those who believe in Him will never perish, but He will raise them up on the last day.

If you have not believed and received Jesus Christ as your Lord, God, and Savior, then now is the time to do it. Confess your sins and agree with God that you are in need of Him. Simply tell God that is what you want to do, and He will give you the gift of eternal life as He gives you His Son—Christ in you, the hope of glory. After you do this, thank God in faith for the gift of eternal life. Then complete your lesson. When you get with your group, tell them what you have done. What rejoicing there will be . . . even as there is in heaven at this very moment! Also jot a note on the response card in the back of this book telling us of your decision so we can help you on your journey with God.

This is why Jesus came to earth—for you, Beloved. Welcome to His forever family. Someday you will see His temple standing again on the threshing floor of Ornan because we are all going to Jerusalem. What a glorious day that will be!

Now read chapter 29. It is such a rich chapter. As you mark key words, mark every occurrence of a phrase that mentions something being *offered willingly (willingly offered, offered so willingly)*.[12] Also mark the word *heart*[13] in a distinctive way—a red heart will do! Then go back and mark *heart* in 28:9.

When you finish, list everything you learn from marking these key words. Then think about what you learn and how it applies to your own life. Record the theme for this last chapter of our study.

You might want to close your study by turning 1 Chronicles 29:10-19 into a prayer.

DAY SEVEN

Store in your heart: 1 Chronicles 29:11,12.
    Read and discuss: 1 Chronicles 21—22:2; 29:1-19; 2 Samuel 24.

Questions for Discussion or Individual Study

1 Chronicles 21–22:2; 2 Samuel 24

- Why did the plague come from the Lord killing 70,000 men of Israel?

  a. Why did David number the people?

  b. Who tried to warn David? What does this tell you about this man? What did this man risk in doing what he did? Do we need more men like this?

  c. How did God feel about it? What did God do?

  d. Why did David choose the punishment he did?

- What did you observe from marking every reference to *the angel of the Lord?*

- What did you learn about the threshing floor of Ornan this week? How does it relate to modern times?

  a. Where was the tabernacle of the Lord when this occurred?

  b. Why David go there?

- What did David recognize in 1 Chronicles 22:1,2?

- What did you learn about David from this chapter? How did David respond once he realized his sin? What lessons can you learn from this for your life?

  a. What did David call his actions?

  b. What do you call your actions when they are acts contrary to the Word and the will of God?

- Who would build the house of the Lord? Why?

1 Chronicles 29:1-19

∾ Where did the funding for the building of the house of the Lord come from?

   a. What did you learn from this passage with respect to David? With respect to the people?

   b. What did you learn from marking every reference to *offering willingly?*

   c. How did David and the people have the means to fund such an expensive project?

   d. What have you learned in all this that you can apply to yourself? To your church? To the work of God around the world?

∾ What did you learn from marking the various references to the heart?

∾ What did you learn about God from this chapter that really caught your attention, captured your heart, or convicted you?

Finally, if there is time...

∾ What did you learn about Solomon this week in your study?

∾ Share one of the most significant observations you've made about David from the book of 2 Samuel and how that observation will or has impacted your life.

THOUGHT FOR THE WEEK

A pestilence resulting in the death of 70,000 Israelites followed the census David ordered. David acted against the warnings of his general, Joab, and independently of his God.

First Chronicles 21:1 explains, "Then Satan stood up against Israel and moved David to number Israel." Second Samuel 24:1 says that "the anger of the LORD burned against Israel."

Throughout our study, we have seen David inquire of the Lord before taking action. Success always followed when David submitted to God's instructions. Failure was certain when he didn't. Even though God had hand-picked David to rule and lead His chosen people, He would not compromise His own standard when David violated it. God is a just God, and the consequences for disobedience apply —to all!

How then can we remain in obedience to God's will? How can we meet His just demands? Is it possible to stand fast when the bottom is falling out? The answer is yes through God's grace. Grace is the gift of undeserved, unmerited favor. Mankind can never earn God's kindness because we are all sinful creatures.

So how, then, can God accept us? By the life of one man, Jesus Christ, God's only begotten Son. Jesus died at the hands of man so that we could be accepted by God. Christ's death brought reconciliation between us and God. Romans 5:8,9 says that "God demonstrates His own love toward us, in that while we were yet sinners, Christ died for us. Much more then, having now been justified by His blood, we shall be saved from the wrath *of God* through Him."

It is only because of Jesus that we are saved from the righteous wrath of God. So let us ask again, "Where do you stand with God? Are you in His wrath or in His Son, Jesus Christ?"

During the course of our study, we asked the question, "Is there security in God, even when the odds are stacked against you?" We hope you can answer with a resounding yes because of what you have learned about God through this study of 2 Samuel and 1 Chronicles.

May you be able to say as David did: "The LORD is my rock and my fortress and my deliverer; my God, my rock, in whom I take refuge; my shield and the horn of my salvation, my stronghold and my refuge; my savior, Thou dost save me from violence. I call upon the LORD, who is worthy to be praised; and I am saved from my enemies" (2 Samuel 22:2-4).

May you walk in the light of these verses from this point on!

2 Samuel at a Glance

Theme of 2 Samuel:

			Chapter Themes	Author:
		1		**Historical Setting:**
		2		
		3		
		4		**Purpose:**
		5		
		6		**Key Words:**
		7		Saul
		8		Jonathan
		9		David
		10		Soloman
		11		Joab
		12		
		13		covenant
		14		Ahithophel
		15		inquired of the
		16		Lord (inquired of God)
		17		the ark (the ark
		18		of God, the ark of the Lord,
		19		the ark of the
		20		covenant of God, the ark of
		21		the Lord God of Israel, the
		22		ark of the
		23		covenant of the Lord)
		24		

NOTES

FIRST SAMUEL

1. NIV; NKJV: *You(r)* KJV: *thee*

2. NIV: *wronged*

3. NIV: *wicked deeds*
   KJV; NKJV: *evil dealings*

4. NIV: *wrongdoing*

5. KJV; NKJV: *trespass*

6. NIV: *violated*

7. NIV: *wrong, crime*

8. NIV: *sin*

9. NIV: also *the ark of the LORD's covenant*

10. NIV: also *the ark*

11. *The International Inductive Study Bible,* produced by Kay Arthur and the staff of Precept Ministries, ©1992, 1993, published by Harvest House Publishers, p. 2101.

12. KJV: *enquired of (at) the LORD (further)*

13. NIV: *asked God, inquiring of God*
    KJV: *enquired of God, asked counsel of God*
    NKJV: also *asked counsel of God*

14. NIV: also *treaty*

15. NIV: *asked God*
    KJV; NKJV: *asked counsel of God*

16. NIV: also *finally*

17. NKJV: *distressing spirit*

18. NIV: *wronged*

19. NIV: *crime*

20. KJV; NKJV: *Doeg, an Edomite*

21. KJV: *transgression*

22. NIV: *born to him in Hebron*
    KJV: *which were born unto him in Hebron*

23. NIV: *these were the children born to him there*
    KJV: *these were born unto him in Jerusalem*

24. NIV: also *the descendants of Kohath*

25. NIV: also *the descendants of Merari*

SECOND SAMUEL

1. KJV: *David enquired of the LORD*

2. NIV: also *the ark of the LORD, the God of Israel*

3. KJV: also *stablish*

4. KJV: *confirmed*

5. NIV: *David pleaded with God*
   KJV: *David therefore besought God*
   NKJV: *David therefore pleaded with God*

6. NIV; KJV; NKJV: also *bring the king back*

7. NIV; NKJV: also *perfect*
   KJV: *upright, perfect*

8. NIV; KJV; NKJV: *perfect*

9. NIV: also *guilt*

10. In the NIV, also mark *an angel.*

11. NIV: *the temple of the LORD*

12. NIV: *gave willingly (the willing response, given willingly)*

13. NIV: also *wholehearted(ly)*

Books in the
International Inductive Study Series

Also by Kay Arthur

How to Study Your Bible

Beloved

His Imprint, My Expression

My Savior, My Friend

God, Are You There?

Lord, Teach Me to Pray in 28 Days

With an Everlasting Love

Israel, My Beloved

Fri 3/22, 4/12

YES, I WANT TO GROW SPIRITUALLY.
TELL ME MORE ABOUT

PRECEPT MINISTRIES INTERNATIONAL

Name _____

Address _____

City_____

State_____ Postal Code _____

Country_____

Daytime phone ( )_____

Email address _____

Fax ( )_____

Evening phone ( )_____

PLEASE SEND ME INFO ON:

❑ Learning how to study the Bible

❑ Bible study material

❑ Radio Programs

❑ TV Programs

❑ Israel Bible Study Tour

❑ Paul's Epistles Study Tour to Greece

❑ Men's Conferences

❑ Women's Conferences

❑ Teen Conferences

❑ Couples' Conferences

❑ Other_____

❑ I want to partner with Precept Ministries

ENCLOSED IS MY DONATION FOR $_____

P.O. Box 182218 • Chattanooga, TN 37422-7218
(800) 763-8280 • (423) 892-6814 • Radio/TV (800) 763-1990
Fax: (423) 894-2449 • www.precept.org • Email: info@precept.org

BUSINESS REPLY MAIL
FIRST-CLASS MAIL   PERMIT NO. 48   CHATTANOOGA TN

POSTAGE WILL BE PAID BY ADDRESSEE

PRECEPT MINISTRIES
P O BOX 182218
CHATTANOOGA TN   37422-9901